Social Class, Gender and Exclusion from School

Rising exclusion rates indicate the continuing marginalisation of many young people in education in the UK. Working-class boys, children living in poverty, and children with additional/special educational needs are among those experiencing a disproportionate rate of exclusion. This book traces the processes of exclusion and alienation from school and relates this to a changing social and economic context.

Jean Kane argues that policy on schooling, including curricular reform, needs to be re-connected to the broad political pursuit of social justice, and presents compelling case studies of excluded pupils, showing the multifaceted identities of pupils, with a particular focus on masculine and feminine identities.

This invaluable contribution to the literature offers an alternative analysis where the social identities of pupils are shown to be tied up with their exclusion from school. Themes investigated include:

- The meanings of school exclusions
- Social class, gender and schooling
- Social identities of excluded pupils
- Negotiating identities in school: moving towards exclusion
- Exclusions and young people's lives
- Improving participation in schooling.

Providing fascinating reading for teachers, social workers, researchers and policymakers, this book considers how educational disadvantage might be addressed through recognition of the gender and class identities of pupils.

Jean Kane is Senior Lecturer in Educational Studies at the University of Glasgow.

Social Class, Gender and Exclusion from School

Jean Kane

This edition published 2011
by Routledge
2 Park Square, Milton Park, Abingdon, Oxon, OX14 4RN

Simultaneously published in the USA and Canada
by Routledge
270 Madison Avenue, New York, NY 10016

Routledge is an imprint of the Taylor & Francis Group, an informa business

© 2011 Jean Kane

Typeset in Garamond by
Pindar NZ, Auckland, New Zealand
Printed and bound in Great Britain by
TJ International Ltd, Padstow, Cornwall

All rights reserved. No part of this book may be reprinted or reproduced or utilised in any form or by any electronic, mechanical, or other means, now known or hereafter invented, including photocopying and recording, or in any information storage or retrieval system, without permission in writing from the publishers.

The right of Jean Kane to be identified as author of this work has been asserted by him/her in accordance with sections 77 and 78 of the Copyright, Designs and Patents Act 1988.

British Library Cataloguing in Publication Data
A catalogue record for this book is available from the British Library

Library of Congress Cataloging-in-Publication Data
Kane, Jean, 1952-
Social class, gender, and exclusion from school / Jean Kane.
  p. cm.
Includes bibliographical references.
 1. Student expulsion—Scotland—Case studies. 2. Children with social disabilities—Education—Scotland—Case studies. 3. Marginality, Social—Scotland—Case studies. I. Title.
  LB3089.4.G7S364 2011
  371.5'4309411—dc22   2010007311

ISBN13: 978-0-415-55301-8 (hbk)
ISBN13: 978-0-415-55302-5 (pbk)
ISBN13: 978-0-203-84501-1 (ebk)

Contents

Acknowledgements vi
List of Abbreviations vii

1 Schooling, participation and exclusion 1

2 The meanings of school exclusions 12

3 Social class, gender and exclusions 34

4 Excluded pupils and their social identities 52

5 Negotiating identities in school: moving towards exclusion 74

6 Exclusion and young people's lives 95

7 Improving participation in schooling 114

8 Conclusion 135

Appendix 1 School exclusions in Scotland 138
Appendix 2 Type and range of data for each case study 140
Bibliography 143
Index 150

Acknowledgements

First, I would like to thank the girls, boys, parents and staff who were involved in this research. Their time, interest and insights were invaluable. A great many people helped with the arrangements for access and data gathering and their support for the research enabled it to go ahead in the first place.

This book came from a PhD study. I owe a great deal to my two supervisors, Sheila Riddell and Nick Watson. Thanks also go to Andy Furlong and Gillean McCluskey for their preparedness to read and comment on drafts of chapters. All of these people gave me the benefit of their expertise, their time and their support. I am very grateful to them. Any errors or misunderstandings in the text are entirely my own responsibility.

Thanks go to Taylor and Francis and the editors who have given permission to reproduce Chapter 9 (pp. 96–106) from an edited collection, Rix, J., Simmons, K., Nind, M. and Sheey, K. (2005) *Policy and Power in Inclusive Education: values into practice*, London, RoutledgeFalmer. Exclusion statistics drawn upon here are subject to Crown copyright status.

In addition, Taylor and Francis have granted permission to reproduce my article 'School Exclusions and Masculine, Working Class Identities', published in *Gender and Education*, 18(6): 673–85. This journal article can be accessed from http://www.informaworld.com

While every effort has been made to trace and acknowledge ownership of copyright material used in this volume, the Publishers will be glad to make suitable arrangements with any copyright holders whom it has not been possible to contact.

The research was sponsored by the Faculty of Education, University of Glasgow. The financial assistance I received is gratefully acknowledged.

Finally, I would like to thank Danny, Eilidh and James who have brightened some difficult times with their interest, encouragement and very practical support.

Abbreviations

AHT	Assistant headteacher
ASNs	Additional support needs
DHT	Deputy headteacher
EIS	Educational Institute of Scotland
FSM	Free school meals
GTC	General Teaching Council
HMIE	Her Majesty's Inspectorate of Education
LA	Local authority
MUD	Moral underclass discourse
NUT	National Union of Teachers
OECD	Organisation for Economic Co-operation and Development
PSD	Personal and social development
PT	Principal teacher
RED	Redistributive Discourse of Exclusion
SEBD	Social, emotional and behavioural difficulties
SED	Scottish Education Department
SEED	Scottish Executive Education Department
SEN	Special educational needs
SID	Social integrationist discourse
SIM	School improvement movement
SOEID	Scottish Office Education and Industry Department

Chapter 1

Schooling, participation and exclusion

Schooling in the UK, and across western education systems, continues to fail some young people. Their marginalised position within education systems is evidenced by rates of formal exclusion from school. Groups such as boys, children living in poverty and children in the care of public authorities are among those experiencing a disproportionate rate of exclusion. Formal exclusion from school is the starting point for this book which traces processes of exclusion and alienation from secondary schools by probing the experience of 20 young people who have been excluded in Scotland. Their exclusion from school is related to their social identities in an effort to understand why some groups fare badly in a school system based on principles of liberal democracy. Although all of the young people discussed here are Scottish, their experience is used to consider school exclusion more widely and in relation to broad welfare and social inclusion policies.

Why do schools exclude some pupils? The obvious answer is because their behaviour is unacceptable to school staff. 'General and persistent disobedience' has been the reason for exclusion most often cited by Scottish schools. In 2007/08, 33 per cent of children were excluded for that reason with a further 26 per cent excluded for verbally abusing a member of staff (Scottish Government, 2009a). In the view of one deputy headteacher (DHT):

> It is shocking that I have to do it. But if he tells a member of staff to f*** off in front of other children . . . Staff are human beings with rights as well. I mean it is totally detrimental to the good order of the school.
> (Deputy headteacher, secondary school)

Less common were exclusions for violent behaviour – 1.6 per cent of exclusions were for physical assault using an improvised weapon and 3.4 per cent were for threatening violence using an improvised weapon (Scottish Government, 2009a). *General and persistent disobedience* is a coverall term – the 'persistent' indicating that the exclusion is a result of cumulative misdemeanours or a failure on the pupil's part to comply with earlier sanctions.

Exclusion is the most serious response to pupil indiscipline available to schools and can vary in length, depending upon the gravity of the offence and the number of times the pupil has been excluded previously. Different kinds of exclusions are further described in Appendix 1. A small minority of pupils, about 3 per cent, experience exclusion with the majority of those pupils excluded on just one occasion in any school year (Scottish Government, 2009a). National and local government monitor exclusions closely with data on exclusions gathered and published annually since 2000. Levels of exclusion in schools and local authorities are taken as an indication of the effectiveness of school discipline policies – Her Majesty's Inspectorate of Education (HMIE) use these data and others in forming judgements about the quality of schools. More widely, the annual publication of exclusion rates is covered in the national media. They are a publicly visible statement of schools' success in managing pupil misbehaviour with plaudits when rates of exclusion decrease, and a 'moral panic' when they rise.

The Scottish Government's exclusion statistics show clear and consistent patterns year-on-year. Exclusions are not evenly spread across the pupil population. Some pupils are far more likely than others to be excluded. Pupils living in poverty, as indicated by their entitlement to free school meals (FSM), were more than twice as likely as other pupils to be excluded in 2006/07 (Scottish Government, 2008). Pupils 'looked after' by the local authority (LA) were five times more likely to be excluded. Boys, in particular, were over-represented. In the 2007/08 session, they accounted for 79 per cent of all exclusions (Scottish Government, 2009a), a proportion of the total which has remained remarkably consistent since exclusion statistics were first published in Scotland in 2000. Over the years of their publication, those exclusion statistics show the gender balance in exclusions to be stable overall with excluded boys outnumbering excluded girls by a 4:1 ratio. Interestingly, the exclusion rates for one other group point up a contradiction for policy on the educational inclusion of pupils with special educational needs (SEN). Where pupils had been assessed or declared as having a disability, the rate of exclusion was considerably higher than for other pupils (Scottish Government, 2009a). And yet, 'mainstreaming' was high on the policy agendas of both Scottish and UK governments.

This book seeks to explain the inequities evident in exclusions statistics by:

- investigating gender, social class and other forms of identity as factors in formal exclusions from school;
- exploring differences in the ways in which schools impacted upon the identities of different social groups and relating those differences to school exclusions;
- considering the means of reducing school exclusions.

Schools are not blamed here for excluding pupils. All four schools considered had highly developed systems of pupil support, as well as staff who were both skilled and compassionate in dealing with some very challenging pupils.

'Problem' behaviour in schools and its remedies have often been located in the pathology of the child/young person (e.g. nurture groups, cognitive behaviour therapy) or in the ethos and organisation of the school (e.g. Assertive Discipline, restorative practices). The focus here is wider than either of these. Young people's lives are considered in and beyond school and the identities they develop are related to their wider social experience.

Official accounts of challenging behaviour and exclusion have neglected the social and cultural factors structuring school exclusion statistics. Instead, remedies have been sought through strategies for school improvement. An alternative analysis is offered here where the social identities of pupils are shown to be tied up with their exclusion from school. Negotiation of particular social class and gender identities in schools results in conflict, disaffection and exclusion. Pupils are shown to be active in negotiations leading to their exclusion. Schools, too, are actively involved in the creation of particular forms of identity for pupils but beyond schooling, possibilities for pupils and schools are limited by a wider social and economic context. Structural inequality means that children and families are differently positioned in relation to schooling and has limited the scope for schools to shape the future lives of pupils. This book considers how educational disadvantage might be addressed through recognition of the gender and class identities of pupils, for example, by enabling increased participation, particularly in curriculum planning.

Exclusions are considered as part of the experience of 20 pupils – 17 boys and 3 girls – in four secondary schools in one LA in the west of Scotland. The main principle governing the selection of the sample was that it should encompass a range of pupil characteristics with the common factor that all had been excluded. The sample was intended to cover the categories which would allow comparison between the identities and experiences of excluded pupils. Those categories included:

- gender
- poverty (as indicated by eligibility for FSM)
- age
- ability in school
- number of previous exclusions
- reasons for exclusion

It was not intended that the case study LA, schools and pupils be representative of the whole population of education authorities, schools and pupils in Scotland. The schools and pupils were selected to enable consideration of only those factors noted earlier within the constraints of permitted access and in negotiation with participating schools. The sample was not constructed to represent a particular gender balance but, as it happened, there were 17 boys and 3 girls, roughly the same gender balance indicated by national exclusion statistics (Scottish Government, 2009a). The pupils were drawn from S1 to

S4, that is, from 12 to 16, the age range of compulsory secondary schooling in Scotland. Case study pupils' experience of exclusion ranged from a single exclusion (two of the three girls were in this category) to multiple and extended periods of exclusion. Nineteen of the pupils were white and Scottish, one boy was black and Scottish. Ethnicity was not an aspect of identity considered in this study in any depth; neither was religion, although one of the schools in the study was a Catholic denominational secondary school. The 2001 census showed 16 per cent of Scotland's population to be Catholic whereas the majority religious group (42 per cent) was Church of Scotland (Presbyterian). The 1918 Education (Scotland) Act provided funding for Catholic and Episcopalian schools, allowing these voluntary establishments to move into the state sector. These 'denominational' schools were able to control religious education and allowed its distinctiveness from the Presbyterianism taught in state 'non-denominational' schools. Catholic denominational and non-denominational schools currently co-exist in the LA – managed sector with 327 Catholic primaries out of a total of 2,164 primary schools in Scotland in 2007. Most Catholic denominational schools are in west, central Scotland; in Glasgow, 40 per cent of the primary pupil population are educated in Catholic schools (McCluskey et al. 2008).

Case study data were gathered in June and September 2003, that is, over two school sessions. The profile of data varied for each case study, depending upon factors such as parental willingness to be interviewed and the depth of information provided by the pupil and other participants. Appendix 2 shows the spread of data sources for each case study. Data were gathered from semi-structured interviews with pupils, parents, teachers and other staff; from focus groups with pupils; from classroom observations; and from documentary material. In all, 105 interviews were conducted in this phase of the research, ranging in length from 1.5 hours to just 10 minutes when some teachers gave a little time at the ends of lessons to comment on what had just passed, before the next class arrived. Pupils were observed in class on 26 occasions, though this was not possible for one of the S4 case study pupils whose attendance had been very poor. All interviews, apart from those with parents, were conducted in the schools. Members of staff in each school, usually DHTs or principal teachers (PTs), helped to organise data gathering, by identifying possible pupil participants and by assisting in arrangements for interviews and observation. Were there disadvantages in using school staff as gatekeepers? It was possible that pupils who had been excluded would feel compelled to participate by the authority of the DHT/PT in the school setting. Care was taken at the start of each interview to explain that participation was voluntary and that the interview was confidential and could be terminated by the pupil at any time. When pupils seemed hesitant or unforthcoming in answering particular questions, they were again given the opportunity to withdraw.

The four secondary schools, Carrick High, Easton High, Hammond High and St Thomas's high schools, were all located in the same LA and were all managed by that LA. That particular LA was composed of very diverse communities and the intention was to consider exclusions in relation to schools serving different pupil populations. For administrative purposes, the LA was divided into four areas, each of them historically, demographically and economically distinct. The plan was to conduct the research in one secondary school in each area but, in the event, it was not possible to gain access to a school in the most affluent, rural area. The LA had 21 secondary schools and collected from them annually statistics for temporary and permanent (removed from the register) exclusions. The key statistic used to identify schools was the number of exclusion incidents reported. Schools also provided information about the number of openings (half-days) lost through exclusions. A ratio of that figure with the number of exclusion incidents would reveal the average length of exclusions in each school. This was thought not to be particularly useful since schools have generally cut back on the length of the period of exclusion. Indeed, during the time when this research was conducted, government guidelines on exclusions (SEED, 2003) were revised to lower the maximum period allowable for temporary exclusion from six weeks to four weeks or twenty school days.

This research did not focus on school differences as a main strand in the analysis of data. Differences are indicated here only to give some sense of the context for the research. The intention was not to evaluate each school's provision in relation to exclusion rates but to consider the broader experience of individual pupils who had been excluded. There was some variation in school size and contrast in entitlement to FSM across the school sample with almost 40 per cent of pupils at Carrick High School registered but only 16.4 per cent registered at Hammond High School, reflecting different employment levels in the communities served by the schools. Consistent with national statistics (Scottish Government, 2009a), rates of exclusion were highest in the school where FSM entitlement was highest; and exclusion rates were lowest in the school with fewest pupils entitled to FSM.

Both Carrick High School and St Thomas's High School were in an area bordering a major city and served two towns with a joint population of 55,182. These towns had much in common with each other and with the neighbouring city – a past in heavy industry and a present battling against economic decline. What was formerly one of the major employers in the area, a large manufacturing company, had reduced its workforce from 5,000 to 100 during the period of this study. Since the demise of the steel and heavy engineering industries, attempts had been made by the LA to encourage new businesses to base themselves in one of a number of business parks surrounding the towns. Easton High School was located in a peripheral housing scheme of the historic county town which in the 2001 census had a population of 48,546 and remained the administrative centre of the authority. There were relatively high rates of social exclusion in the communities served by the school. Hammond High School served what was once called a 'new town', built in the late 1950s from the original village and provided homes to young families from the nearby city. Its population of 73,796 was socially mixed and had a high level of economic activity. This area provided 30 per cent of the jobs available within the whole LA. Its industry in the main was light, electronics industry but central and local government offices were also based here. The school's intake was reasonably affluent with some middle class and professional families using the school, although, generally, the community was affluent working class. In that respect, the school was the most advantaged of the four case study schools.

Carrick High School was a non-denominational secondary school serving an area of significant social exclusion near the boundary with the neighbouring city. Its exclusion rates were the highest of the four schools. Almost 40 per cent of pupils were entitled to FSM, the highest level in the sample. The school was housed in 1960s buildings and had a range of facilities including, for example, a large assembly hall and stage. The buildings were no longer in good repair and it was anticipated that refurbishments would be carried out under the LA's public/private partnership financial arrangement.

St Thomas's High School was a Catholic denominational school near to Carrick High School and covering some of the same local communities, but drawing upon a wider and more socially diverse area. The school was housed in modern buildings and had extensive playing fields. St Thomas's was the largest of the four case study schools. Almost 24 per cent of its pupils were entitled to FSM.

St Thomas's High School is a Catholic denominational school and its relatively low rates of exclusion contrast with exclusion rates at Carrick High School. Commentators have noted the relative success of these publicly funded denominational schools as measured by hard indicators such as examination results, attendance and exclusion statistics. This has been attributed to Catholic schools having a better ethos arising from a clearly articulated value system to which the whole school community subscribes. School effectiveness and school improvement research has indeed underlined the importance of a unifying value system in contributing to successful schools. However, there may be other factors contributing to the success of denominational schools. Catholic schools are fewer than non-denominational schools and tend to serve a wider catchment area. For many pupils more effort is required to opt for Catholic education and some families, those with fewest resources, take the easiest course and send their children to the nearest school. The effect is that a self-selection process operates with some pupils from Catholic primary schools opting out of (or never opting into) the associated Catholic secondary school.

Easton High School was located in a housing scheme in the town which is the administrative centre of the LA. At the time of the research 21.5 per cent of its pupils were entitled to FSM. The school was about to merge with the secondary school which served a nearby town. Although this was a merger, the combined school would be in a new building on the site of the other school and so the staff in Easton were fearful of the impending upheaval and insecurity with regard to their own posts.

Hammond High School is a co-educational, non-denominational secondary school. In the school 16.5 percent of its pupils were entitled to FSM. The exclusion rate was the lowest of the four schools. Hammond High School itself would not be significantly affected by the LA's plans under the public/private partnership arrangements. The school was housed in well-maintained 1960s style accommodation.

Prior to the case study phase of the research, a series of 17 key informant interviews was conducted with a range of stakeholders including Scottish Executive and LA staff involved in developing and overseeing guidance on exclusions; school managers implementing exclusions; and pupils with experience of exclusion. During this first phase of the research the intention was to establish the philosophy, aims, functioning, effectiveness and consistency of exclusions policy at national, local and school levels. Relevant policy documentation from all agencies was scrutinised, compared and contrasted. It was recognised that operational policy could differ considerably from written statements. Policy was recognised as dynamic and, no matter how conscientious an organisation might be in committing its agreed policies to paper, these were likely to change almost as soon as they were embodied in text. There was, too, the possibility that written policies were interpreted and implemented differently by different readers. For both of these reasons, I anticipated that the policy perspectives offered by key people in schools, LAs and Scottish Executive Education Department (SEED) would yield richer (and probably more conflicting) data than would be gleaned from an analysis of the documentation alone. Key informants were a main source of data about policy and practice in exclusions. In addition to professional perspectives on exclusions, the views of young people themselves were gathered. This perspective was an important one for the study during the case study phase but it was hoped that by including interviews with young people as key informants, broad issues of policy and practice would emerge which were different from those highlighted by professionals. Access to the young people was arranged through the agency of their school. All were boys although the request to the school had not stipulated this gender representation. Chapter 2, which deals with the various meanings of exclusion, draws on key informant data. The range of interviews conducted represented the perspectives of all of the main parties involved in exclusions – pupils, teachers, administrators and policymakers – and it was anticipated that this first part of the research would identify issues and questions not considered in the original research proposal. The views of key informants were used to refine the focus of subsequent fieldwork.

The standpoint of the researcher has shaped this research. I was a secondary-school teacher for nearly 20 years and latterly had responsibility for excluding first- and second-year pupils. I excluded pupils with awareness of the likely negative consequences for them in the present and into the future, but also feeling that I had no other option at the time. Parents, almost always young women, would sometimes ask what good the exclusion would do. For those women and their children the answer was none at all. My own experience was very useful in this research in gaining access to schools and in securing the help of school staff in organising data gathering but it has also influenced my attitudes when analysing data and drawing conclusions for I am sympathetic to schools. My aim in this book is not to find fault with individual schools but to appraise policy which has failed to tackle the broader educational exclusion of numbers of young people in Scotland.

My own background is working class. Unlike the young people discussed further on, I did well out of LA schools in the 1960s and was able to go to university with a grant. Times have changed for the working class, culturally as well as economically. In considering the experience of pupils' excluded from school, and their social class and gender identities, I want to relate education to wider social inequalities.

To answer the question which opened this chapter – Why are pupils excluded? – it would seem from newspaper coverage that pupils are excluded because this is seen by teachers and by a wider public as a necessary response to indiscipline, necessary to the continuing education of other pupils, perhaps even to the welfare of pupils and teachers. Drawing on an apocalyptic vision, the *Sunday Herald* (16/1/05), commenting on discipline in secondary schools, demonstrated how indiscipline had been constructed as a function of the government's social inclusion policy. The inclusion of pupils with learning difficulties or physical disabilities was generously applauded, while the inclusion of those with social and behavioural problems was deprecated in strong terms.

The practice of exclusion, though, is at odds with the thrust of social policy. Social factors such as gender and social class, which structure the Scottish Executive's statistical data, are invisible in policy and in related strategies. It is a contention of this study that exclusions are to be understood as bound up with the processes by which particular class and gender identities are negotiated in school settings. The antecedents of this work lie in an older sociology of education which sought to understand class-related inequalities in the education systems of the UK. It is argued that the same inequalities are manifested currently in exclusion and other school statistics. This investigation is informed by a view of social justice as embracing social and cultural, as well as economic factors. Attention to those social and cultural factors would lead to a more radical view of schools and schooling in the endeavour to provide more socially just outcomes. A brief outline of subsequent chapters is as follows:

Chapter 2 The meanings of school exclusions

This chapter explores the multiple and conflicting meanings of exclusion in policy, in practice and in the experience of those who have been excluded from school. Policy and procedures for exclusions in Scotland are outlined. In themselves, they are clear but they create contradictions with other educational policies, for example, the inclusion of pupils with additional support needs (ASNs) and with wider social inclusion policy. Other layers of meaning are revealed through key informant interviews. Exclusions are seen to be experienced overwhelmingly as a punishment by young people and their families and yet punishment does not feature in official accounts of exclusion. The specific mechanism of school exclusion is related to dominant political ideologies of social exclusion, and to welfare regimes which marginalise and stigmatise. Schools have been seen as a forum where institutionalised disadvantage might be addressed, even where social class reproduction might be challenged. This chapter sees the practice of exclusion as indicating schools are a long way from fulfilling either of these functions.

Chapter 3 Social class, gender and exclusions

The theoretical approaches of this study are explained. Theories of class culture and gender identities are discussed, their applications in previous school-based research indicated (Reay, 1998; Ball, 2003; Skeggs, 2004), and their relevance to understanding school exclusions considered. The cultural dimension of social class has been to the fore in the class analyses of sociologists. Using Bourdieu's conceptual tools of habitus, capital and field, class cultural theorists focus on class processes and practices, the everyday workings of social class, developing conceptualisations that move beyond the economic and exchange (Reay, 2006: 289). Although some of this empirical work is related to school and classroom processes (Plummer, 2000; Reay and Wiliam, 1999), Reay (2006) argues that education policy and initial teacher education routinely present classrooms as classless. This view is borne out by Scottish Executive policy on behaviour, *Better Behaviour – Better Learning* (SEED, 2000a) which mentions neither social class nor gender although government statistics are clearly structured by both. The reasons for the disproportionate exclusion from school of certain groups will be sought in class cultural understandings and also in theories of gender identities. A body of school-based research, highly theorised, has illuminated how, and to what effect, masculinities and femininities are negotiated in school settings. Chapter 3 will draw upon this work, paying particular attention to the relationship between inclusion/exclusion and the processes by which class and gendered identities are negotiated in school settings – processes bound up with working-class experience of compulsory education.

Chapter 4 Excluded pupils and their social identities

Using data from 20 case studies of excluded pupils, this chapter explores the multifaceted identities of pupils, with a particular focus on masculine and feminine identities. Alignments and oppositions within gender relations are illustrated and analysed and gender identities are shown to be intersected by other forms of identity such as sectarian identities and particular 'youth culture' identities such as Neds, which may be seen as an intentional cultural expression of social exclusion.

Chapter 5 Negotiating identities in school: moving towards exclusion

This chapter illustrates how boys and girls negotiate particular identities in school settings. These identities link to the reasons why pupils were excluded, and to pupils' overall engagement with schooling. Some negotiations, of working-class masculinities in particular, are shown to be tied up with oppositional behaviour and school exclusion. Teachers are shown to be active in the negotiation of pupil identities and to use ability labels such as 'bright' and 'learning difficulties' as part of those negotiations.

Chapter 6 Exclusion and young people's lives

This chapter considers the relationship between exclusion from school and the wider circumstances of young peoples' lives. Empirical data is used to show how poverty undermined engagement with schooling and exacerbated chances of pupils being excluded. Exclusions are shown to cause additional pressure on fragile family relationships and to have an alienating effect on families' relationships with schools. Consideration is given to the longer-term effect of exclusions with pupils' constructions of their own futures demonstrating their insecurity and resignation.

Chapter 7 Improving participation in schooling

Implications of the previous three chapters are considered in relation to the organisation of schooling in UK education systems. Excluded pupils and their families are seen to be ill-positioned in relation to education because of structural inequalities. Broader 'welfare' approaches emerging from social inclusion policy are seen to be capable of supporting pupils on the margins of schooling but not of moving them into the mainstream processes of schooling. Responses to challenging behaviour based upon school improvement strategies are seen to have limited success. Ways of increasing participation of 'hard-to-reach' families are discussed. The experience of some pupils pointed towards greater choice and flexibility in the curriculum as a step towards increased participation and a means of maintaining connection to schooling.

Chapter 8 Conclusion

Exclusions are seen as a function of gendered and 'classed' experience of school. This chapter will consider class cultural identities as impacting on pupils' experience of schooling but as having been neglected in policy, teacher education and curriculum provision.

Chapter 2

The meanings of school exclusions

On the surface, exclusion from school is a puzzling phenomenon. Policy emphasises inclusion, participation, the importance of education and skills, and yet each year thousands of vulnerable young people are excluded from school. This paradox is at the heart of this chapter where school exclusions are considered against a broader background of public policy. The practice of exclusion from school, and the patterns evident in exclusion statistics, are both used to probe policy frameworks which foster social inclusion. But exclusion from school also has meaning for those who are excluded and their families, and for those who administer exclusions. This policy analysis is related to the experience of those most closely involved and affected by exclusion, using interview data from pupils, local authority (LA) officers, headteachers and policymakers.

Inclusive education has been a hallmark of schools policy in UK education systems for more than two decades and yet it remains problematic with concerns coming from a number of quarters (Allan, 2008). A range of constituencies continue to experience exclusion from education. Exclusion itself takes multiple forms. Some pupils exclude themselves either by truanting or by withdrawing from school and classroom processes. Other pupils are excluded for all practical purposes because they are unable to participate in the curriculum or even to be involved socially in the playground. A third group is formally excluded by school staff because their behaviour has been judged to be incompatible with the maintenance of good order in the school. Discussion here focuses on this last group – those who have been formally excluded from school – while recognising that all forms of exclusion are worth examining in a policy context which emphasises inclusion. Indeed, it could be argued that the processes of inclusion might best be understood by considering the experience of those who are excluded.

Formal exclusions in Scotland are carefully monitored by central government. At the end of the 1990s an obligation was placed on LAs to collect and report exclusions data on an annual basis (SOEID, 1998a). In July 2000, the result of the first annual survey of school exclusions was published (SEED, 2000b) and the results of subsequent surveys have been published annually since then. The statistics have been structured by a range of social factors:

gender, stage of schooling, poverty indicators (free school meals), looked after by LA and special educational needs (SEN). While the availability of national data has been welcomed, fears have been expressed about under-reporting of exclusions by schools (Munn *et al.*, 2000; Stirling, 1996; Blyth and Milner, 1996). It is possible for schools to misrepresent the level of exclusions in a number of ways, for example, by using informal or 'internal' exclusion where pupils are retained on school premises but do not attend ordinary lessons. In addition, where there have been a number of previous incidents, parents may be persuaded to move the pupil to another school in the interests of the pupil himself (Blyth and Milner, 1996) but also preventing the need for the school to record the event as a formal exclusion. The incentive for schools to under-report exclusions has been attributed to government target-setting in the area of exclusions (Munn *et al.*, 2000; Parsons, 1999). Target-setting may have pressurised schools into under-reporting exclusions but it also failed to stem the rising tide of reported exclusions. In Scotland in 2003/04, the year during which target-setting was abandoned, exclusions rose by 7 per cent (SEED, 2005). In England, target-setting did reduce exclusions but commentators (Hayden, 1997; Parsons, 1999) saw the reductions achieved by the target-setting exercise in one area as outweighed by the overall pressure to meet attainment targets and by the exclusionary culture thus created in classrooms and schools. This is further discussed later on.

Around 3 per cent of Scottish pupils are excluded annually. The demography of exclusion statistics overall has varied little year-on-year and so it is possible to take one session as illustrative of overall patterns (Scottish Government, 2009a). For example, in the 2007/08 school session, 20,600 different pupils were excluded with the total number of exclusions amounting to 39,717, of which 164 were exclusions leading to removal from the register of the school concerned. Of the 20,600 pupils who were excluded, 60 per cent were excluded on only one occasion, 19 per cent were excluded on two occasions and 21 per cent, that is about 4,000 pupils, experienced multiple exclusions in the course of one school session. Exclusion rates vary greatly between sectors with 83 per cent of exclusions arising in secondary schools, 14 per cent in primary schools and 3 per cent in special schools. Exclusion rates rise throughout Primary 1 to Secondary 2 (13-year-olds), peaking for 14-year-olds in Secondary 3. Pupils living in areas of multiple deprivation, those with additional support needs (ASNs) and those looked after by the LA all had higher exclusion rates than other pupils. Boys accounted for 79 per cent of exclusions in the 2007/08 session and the overall gender ratio of 4 male exclusions to 1 female exclusion has been a consistent feature of published statistics. In Scotland, while the rate of exclusion varied between schools and LAs, the LAs with the highest rates of exclusion served urban communities.

Statistical data have shown the link between school exclusions and poverty. Previous statistics (SEED, 2005) showed that children registered for free school meals (FSM) in Scotland were two and a half times more likely to be excluded.

FSM were used as a key indicator of poverty and were commonly correlated with attainment and attendance, as well as with exclusions. More recent government statistics link cases of exclusion to the top and bottom 20 per cent of the Scottish Index of Multiple Deprivation (Scottish Government, 2009b). In the top 20 per cent of areas covered by that index, there are 15 cases of exclusion recorded for every 1,000 pupils; in the bottom 20 per cent there are 117 cases recorded for every 1,000 pupils. The cumulative effect on individuals of exclusions is difficult to gauge from official statistics. For example, although statistics (Scottish Government, 2009a) show that 21 per cent of those excluded in 2003/04 were excluded three times or more during that session, the duration of their exclusions is not shown. It is not possible, therefore, to quantify the total number of school days lost to individual pupils in that session. This is unfortunate when the repeated and lengthening exclusion of some individuals is likely to indicate a higher level of social exclusion than that prevailing among the 60 per cent of excluded pupils in Scotland who were excluded just once during that same session (Scottish Government, 2009a). In England, concern about the repeated exclusion of a number of pupils led to the amendment of the exclusion regulations (Education [No. 2] Act, 1993) by the Standards and Framework Act (DFEE, 1998), which limited the aggregate number of fixed-term exclusions possible for an individual pupil to 45 days per school session. While the specification of a ceiling to temporary exclusions might be desirable, Macrae et al. (2003) point out that 9 weeks is a significant proportion of time in a school year of 40 weeks. In addition, exclusions have been noted as carrying a high cost for local communities, as well as for the education and well-being of pupils excluded. Tomlinson (2005) points to the number of burglaries committed by 10- to 16-year-olds during the school day.

Schools policy: inclusion and exclusion

Exclusions occur within a policy and legal framework which emphasises school inclusion. In common with other western education systems, in UK education systems, the intention has been to see a larger number of children educated in mainstream schools, while still recognising the importance of special units and schools for a small number of children with more complex or profound needs (Riddell and Banks, 2001). The Standards in Scotland's Schools, etc. Act (Scotland) (Scottish Executive, 2000) was landmark legislation which established the 'presumption of mainstream' for all of Scotland's children. Section 15 of that Act requires that provision for pupils be made in mainstream schools unless an exception could be made under any one of three stipulated categories. The 2000 Act shifted the balance towards placement in mainstream schools; alternative arrangements were to be made only in exceptional circumstances. The exceptions applied where placement in mainstream school:

- would not be suited to the ability or aptitude of the child;

- would be incompatible with the provision of efficient education for the children with whom the child would be educated;
- would result in unreasonable public expenditure being incurred which would not normally be incurred.

These categories of exception offer very wide gateways into special settings for parents and local authorities seeking such an option.

Pupils with challenging behaviour, sometimes termed social, emotional and behavioural difficulties (SEBD) in Scotland, were sometimes recognised as having SEN and sometimes not. The imprecision in the use of the term SEBD reflects ambiguity in identifying who has and who does not have these difficulties. The term SEBD has been used in Scotland since the abolition of statutory categories of disability in the early 1980s. Its use to denote a sub-category of SEN has resulted in anomalies in responses to pupils whose behaviour is challenging. This group was among a number of new groups whose particular needs were recognised in legislation enacted by the Scottish Parliament, the Education (Additional Support for Learning) (Scotland) Act 2004 and 2009. Pupils with SEBD were placed within a new framework of provision for pupils with SEN also including gifted and very able pupils, asylum-seekers and children belonging to particular cultural groups such as the Gypsy/Traveller community. Central to the changes were more planned and coordinated support for a wider range of pupils both in school and, for some, extending to other services beyond schools. New ways of organising provision were claimed to be more encompassing and more equitable. The whole group recognised as having ASNs was larger and all pupils within this group were to have an IEP and their needs were to be met from the school's own resources. A much smaller group of pupils were entitled to a Co-ordinated Support Plan (CSP) which drew upon services and resources beyond the school, for example, of speech and occupational therapists. Riddell (2002) comments that, although this arguably better reflected the changing make up of modern society, the group of pupils with ASNs was a potentially large group of children and young people, many of whom may require intensive support at various times during their educational career and beyond. The resource implications therefore were likely to be significant.

Will the acknowledgement that SEBDs merit additional support impact upon the exclusion of those pupils whose behaviour is challenging? Not necessarily – as well as being framed by discourses of SEN (more recently in Scotland, ASNs), challenging behaviour has been constructed as deviance and as a function of the pathology of the school to be tackled through school improvement methods. Often all three constructions of challenging behaviour are co-present in particular schools – disruption and challenging behaviour are construed as deviance, as symptomatic of a SEN and as indicative of a need for school development. Commentators have traced these alternative – and sometimes competing – discourses of SEBD/challenging behaviour in the language and professional practices operating around behaviour support and exclusions (MacLeod and Munn, 2004; Watson, 2005; Maguire *et al.* 2005). For example, it is argued that there are tensions between viewing some young people as having 'needs' and others as requiring correction, between policy and school responses framed by welfare and others by 'the will to punish' (Parsons, 2005). The educational inclusion movement advocated school development as the means of ensuring that pupils with SEN would be fully included in all aspects of school life (Booth *et al.* 2000; Skidmore, 2004; Thomas and Vaughan, 2004). A focus on the pathology of the school was seen to be more beneficial for the pupil than one which identified challenging behaviour as a problem within the child (Thomas and Glenny, 2000). The school improvement approach to managing behaviour has brought about improvement to schools' inclusive capacity but it fails to acknowledge the social and cultural identities of pupils, for example, in seeing gender, and the negotiation of particular gendered identities, as factors in pupils' engagement with schooling.

The Scottish Executive in the explanatory document that accompanied the Bill, *Moving Forward! Additional Support for Learning* (Scottish Executive, 2003) explained their vision as 'We wish to see an education system that is inclusive, welcomes diversity and provides an equal opportunity for all our children to develop their personality, skills and abilities to their fullest potential' (Scottish Executive, 2003).

This aim would seem to be a long way from realisation for those groups who experience school exclusion in its many forms. Policy is never monolithic but the tension between two aspects of policy – inclusion and exclusion – seems particularly stark. In probing this contradiction further, the discussion will turn to themes of inclusion and exclusion in a wider policy context.

Policy frameworks and welfare regimes

The practice of exclusion from school was inconsistent with, not just policies of educational inclusion, but also with wider social inclusion policy (Maguire *et al.* 2005: 140). For New Labour, school exclusion both manifested and exacerbated social exclusion and a reduction in school exclusions was a means of pursuing social inclusion (Scottish Executive, 1999). This contradiction between school discipline policy, which included the use of exclusion, and social inclusion policy was particularly pointed because the young people most vulnerable to social exclusion were also most likely to be excluded from school. A range of policy initiatives addressed the relationship between educational and wider social exclusion with the delivery of integrated services to young people and families emerging as a hallmark strategy of social inclusion. The aim was pursued through the New Community Schools initiative (Scottish Office, 1998) and in Scotland is now embodied in a range of initiatives under the banner of *Getting it Right for Every Child* (Scottish Government, 2008). Key themes relate to the engagement of pupils, families and communities, in addition to the coordination of management and service provision. Integrated service provision was very challenging for schools. Commentators (O'Connor and Lewis, 1999; Riddell and Tett, 2001) criticised the capacity of LA services, as they were structured and operated, to provide the integrated support viewed as necessary to promote the social inclusion of marginalised children and families. But criticisms of social inclusion policies went well beyond their influence on the educational sphere.

The term 'social exclusion' has featured prominently in policy discussion in the UK and in Europe. The factors which characterise social exclusion are noted by Silver (1994) as long-term or repeated unemployment, family instability, social isolation and the decline of neighbourhood and social networks. Alvey and Brown (2001) distinguish between the notion of social exclusion and poverty, arguing that social exclusion covers both the causes and effects of poverty, discrimination and disadvantage. 'Social exclusion' is used to describe the industrial, social and economic changes experienced through the 1980s and 1990s and which resulted in marked deterioration in the quality of life available to large numbers of people.

Although influential on the social policy of a number of European governments, understandings of the term 'social inclusion' are by no means in harmony. Macrae *et al.* (2003) comment that there is a limited consensus of what is meant by the term. It is argued (Viet-Wilson, 1998; Millbourne, 2002; Macrae *et al.* 2003) that some 'weak' versions of the concept are merely attempts to attach the excluded more firmly to established social structures whereas 'strong' versions critique the power relations which result in exclusion. The former version offers a *'safer, top-down version of inclusion which, at its worst, may well be based on a pathology of the poor or disenfranchised'* (Macrae et al. 2003: 90). The latter, 'strong' conceptualisation challenges the existing and exclusionary social order and views the inclusion of the poor and disenfranchised as necessarily entailing change in that order. By this account, social inclusion policies encompass a means of addressing inequality as well as a way of tackling poverty and disengagement. The most comprehensive critiques have noted that social inclusion policies have displaced a socialist commitment to re-distribution of wealth in the UK, and have done so during a period of increasing inequality (Levitas, 2005; Tomlinson, 2005).

It is hard to detect in UK's social inclusion policies any element which might impact on existing social structures, or on the relative wealth of each social stratum. Welfare states are concerned with *'the production and distribution of social well-being'* (Esping-Andersen, 1990: 1) but these aims have been undermined by the scale of post-war unemployment. Tomlinson (2005) argues further that the 1945 commitment to creating and sustaining a welfare state has diminished in the 60-year period since, when UK society has come to be dominated by private enterprises and competitive markets, forcing numbers of people to rely on welfare. This in itself has been held to account for a 'backlash' against the poorest sections of the population by taxpayers fearful that welfare provision is too stretched or suspicious that claimants are ineligible. Esping-Andersen (1990: 33) rejects the argument that backlashes against welfare provision are fuelled when public expenditure burdens become too heavy for taxpayers. On the contrary, he argues, opposition to welfare provision has been at its weakest when welfare spending has been heaviest:

> The risks of welfare state backlash depend not on spending but on the class character of welfare states. Middle-class welfare states, be they social democratic (as in Scandinavia) or corporatist (as in Germany), forge middle-class loyalties. In contrast, the liberal, residualist welfare states found in the United States, Canada, and, increasingly, Britain, depend upon the loyalties of a numerically weak and often politically residual social stratum.
>
> (Esping-Andersen, 1990: 33)

The period since 1945 then may have seen not a move away from a welfare state in the UK but a shift in the kind of welfare regime operating, where welfare itself is stigmatised. Welfare regimes *have* the capacity to reduce inequality – indeed, Esping-Andersen (1990: 180) notes that equality was what welfare regimes were supposed to be about. Equality is assisted by welfare regimes which enable a high level of 'de-commodification' of labour power, that is, by enabling people to enjoy security and well-being independently of the nature and extent of their participation in the labour market. In the UK, the decline and failure of welfare is signaled by its inability to ameliorate inequalities by enabling a high enough level of de-commodification. Social stratification is exacerbated by a welfare regime with 'one group at the bottom primarily reliant on stigmatizing relief; one group in the middle predominantly reliant on social insurance; and, finally, one privileged group capable of deriving its main welfare from the market' (Esping-Andersen,1990: 64–65).

The apparent paradox between policy which emphasises inclusion but continues to exclude begins to look false: social inclusion policies are not at odds with exclusion. Rather, they have helped to solidify the economic identity of one group as needy and different from other groups, set apart by virtue of its reliance upon government welfare.

Cultural and political identities, too, have been changed during the second half of the twentieth century. The nature of employment altered; the 'post-industrial' phase of capitalist economies saw new jobs emerge, previously scarce jobs increase and the need for skilled and unskilled manual labour go into steep decline. Alongside that decline was a loosening of class-based solidarities, including a weakening of the power and influence of working-class organisations, principally the trade unions (Rattansi and Pheonix, 1997: 123). Trade union membership peaked in 1979 and declined through the 1980s and early 1990s (Barratt, 2009). The impact of these and other changes is detectable in schooling. Traditional identities have been disembedded, although original sources of inequality remain intact. Collective identities have been weakened and, for young people, school to work transitions are experienced individually (Furlong and Cartmel, 2007: 13).

The distance from characterising difference to stigmatising it can be a short one. Commentators have detected in social inclusion policy a tendency to designate some groups as a problem. Levitas (2005) delineates three discourses of social exclusion – moral underclass discourse (MUD), social integrationist discourse (SID) and a redistributive discourse of exclusion (RED) – and argues that, while SID has dominated New Labour policy, the co-presence of MUD has ensured an emphasis on changing behaviour *through a mixture of sticks and carrots – manipulation of welfare benefits, sanctions for non-compliance and intensive social work with individuals* (Levitas, 2005). Levitas comments that MUD identifies particular groups as a problem for social order and responds with behavioural, and often repressive, solutions to that problem. This point is picked up further on in discussing the experience of those excluded from school.

So what happened to schooling?

How has wider structural change during the second half of the twentieth century impacted on schooling? From the 1980s government initiatives in education have utilised the concept of school improvement in pursuit of objectives such as raising attainment, increasing educational inclusion and reducing exclusion (Ainscow, 1993). Gray *et al.* (1999), referring to the education system in England and Wales, point out that the school improvement discourse has had a striking impact on policy approaches to schools:

> In less than a decade the educational system has moved from a position where changes in performance from one year to the next were so small as barely to excite comment to one where 'improvement' has not merely been expected but demanded.
>
> (Gray *et al.* 1999: 1)

In Scotland, as well as in education systems across the world, the school improvement movement (SIM) has had an impact on policy and on legislation (e.g. Scottish Executive, 1999; SEED, 2000a). It has provided a framework for judging schools and a means of seeking change. The terminology of school improvement pervades official publications and popular discourse – 'target-setting', 'excellence', 'performance', 'improving' (and its converse 'failing') are everywhere. The SIM is not without its critics. It has been argued that it manifests:

- an over-concern with outcomes and a neglect of processes such as learning and teaching (Mortimore, 1999: 32);
- a focus on too narrow a range of outcomes (Mortimore, 1999);

- a disregard for issues of equity through its treatment of schools as 'hermetically sealed units' (Morley and Rassool, 1999: 83; Slee *et al.* 1998); and
- a tortuous research route to findings which are just common sense (Sammons, 1999: 46).

In spite of these criticisms, it is easy to see why the SIM has had such an impact on education policy and on practice in schools. While it has long been recognised that social class is the main determinant of educational outcomes, inequality has not been susceptible to change, not as a result of social inclusion policy and certainly not as a result of schooling. The appeal of the SIM is its promise that action, albeit in the limited sphere of the school, can result in change for the better. It provides a way of challenging poor educational attainment without the need for wealth redistribution. The SIM body of research has had great appeal for governments seeking to improve educational outcomes, even though SIM researchers themselves have cautioned against a narrowing of the range of processes and outcomes to be considered and thereby judging schools only on what can be easily measured. Mortimore (1999), in replying to criticism that school effectiveness research has wrongly assumed that all pupils want what the school has to offer, agreed that 'most school effectiveness studies do start with the assumption that students want to succeed. If this, for any reason, is not the case, then many of the strategies of school improvement are likely to fail' (Mortimore, 1999: 327).

That SIM-based strategies have failed numbers of pupils has become increasingly obvious in Scotland and elsewhere. Inequitable outcomes of schooling are a matter of concern. Such was the message of a review conducted under the auspices of the Organisation for Economic Co-operation and Development, *Quality and Equity of Schooling in Scotland* (Teese *et al.* 2007). The report commended the strong overall performance of Scottish schools in relation to other developed countries while commenting upon achievement gaps in primary schools and uneven participation and completion rates in secondary schools. The problem for Scotland, the review group indicated, was not unequal access to good schools but unequal capacity to use good schools well (Teese *et al.* 2007: 59). Inequities in deriving benefit from schooling are apparent in differential support for the post-school destinations of pupils:

> A largely academic curriculum until recently has made few concessions to the need to see where school leads and why scholarly effort is important. More successful students enjoy greater certainty, and they can commit themselves more fully to schoolwork because there is a clear institutional goal: school leads to university. But for weaker learners, there is considerable uncertainty.
>
> (Teese *et al.* 2007: 89)

In England, the development of quasi-market systems which fostered competition between schools was more enthusiastically pursued than in Scotland and with greater exclusionary effect. Local authorities retained a central role in the management of schools in Scotland, lessening (to some extent) competition between schools in the same area. The by-words in the English school system of 'choice' and 'competition' were heard less frequently in Scotland and the pressure of performance was seen to be heightened in comparison with the Scottish experience. For example, the substantial rise in exclusions in England in the 1990s was attributed to the pressure on schools to produce strong academic results overall, with the introduction of published league tables of examination results and other indicators of performance in schools creating *a climate less likely to be sympathetic to children not only producing no positive contribution to these indicators, but who may also prevent others from doing so* (Hayden, 1997: 8).

Beyond school how does social exclusion impact on young people's experience of school? The link between educational exclusion and social exclusion goes beyond the impact of formal exclusion from school. The multiple effects of poverty, for example, physical and mental health problems, are acknowledged as having an exclusionary effect on young people's engagement with schooling and on their life chances. For example, Cogan (2004: 191), in a study of the impact of parents' mental health problems on their children, identified four ways in which children's schooling was affected:

- through fights and upsets at home distracting them from homework or exam preparation;
- missing school or being late for school because a parent needed them;
- lack of routine and structure at home;
- inability to concentrate when at school through worry.

Commentators have discussed the impact of poverty on the lives of children and particularly on their experience of school (Reay, 1998; Ridge, 2005). Its exclusionary effect on young people has been identified; the economic restrictions of some pupils' lives preventing full participation. For example, a number of school social activities, such as excursions, demand expenditure. In addition, Ridge points to institutional practices such as the requirement for uniform and particular kinds of equipment as causing pressure for some school pupils. Sometimes, these requirements are concealed from families through children's desire to protect parents from knowledge of their children's experience of poverty. Thus, poverty prevents full participation in schooling and has been noted by a number of commentators as a factor in withdrawal or self-exclusion from school, forms of exclusion particularly affecting girls. Young people's own views of the impact of poverty are still relatively under-researched:

> Although we have an abundance of statistical data that can tell us how many children are poor and for how long . . . we still have little understanding

of what poverty means for children, or how they interpret its presence in their lives.

(Ridge, 2005: 23)

Poverty contributes to the wider social alienation of those experiencing it. The rights and responsibilities of citizenship are fundamentally affected by inequality (Levitas, 2005: 13). The link between exclusion from school and broader factors in social exclusion is further explored later on using data from key-informant interviews. The question is posed as to whether these two factors exist in a causal relationship or whether both are alike in being just symptoms of deeper, structural inequalities in society. The discussion here links to a long-standing educational debate about the relative influence of school processes and social class factors on the attainment and long-term well-being of young people. Whitty (2001: 287) characterises the UK government's social inclusion policy as ignoring the strong messages from sociological research about the importance of social class in educational achievement, and favouring instead the 'new sociology of education' with its emphasis on school effectiveness and school improvement. Whitty (2001) argues that this approach continues to fail the working class and, further, that a genuinely socially inclusive strategy would tackle the self-exclusion of the middle-class from state education as well as the social exclusion of the working class. The government's emphasis on social and cultural factors could be said to distract attention from the economic policies which have created increasing inequality in contemporary society. The new rhetoric, it might be said, simply masks very old problems of poverty and inequality.

The meaning of exclusion for excluded young people and their families

Exclusions have meaning in the experience of those who are excluded and their families, as well as for those who administer exclusions. To understand school exclusions better, 17 in-depth interviews were conducted with a series of 'experts', including four young people who had been excluded. Their views are given some prominence in the analysis here because they offered a perspective distinct from other participants, all of whom were professionals. There were differences between the accounts of professionals but greater differences between pupil and professional accounts, although, on certain points there was agreement across those interviewed. Each participant, by virtue of her/his personal or professional experience, was able to illuminate issues of policy and practice for the researcher; allow the identification of strengths and difficulties in current policy; and to assist in directing the main fieldwork in schools towards problematic issues. Exclusion emerged not just in the technical sense of formal exclusion from school but as located in broader experiences of inclusion and exclusion in schooling, and of affiliation and identity beyond schooling. The themes shaping the analysis and providing the organisers for this section were:

- exclusion as punishment
- effects on young people who were excluded
- differential impact of exclusions
- consistency and fairness
- effectiveness of exclusions.

These themes are considered here in that order, beginning with discussion of exclusion as a form of punishment.

Exclusion as punishment

The responses of the key informants were contradictory in that officials and professionals did not include punishment in the range of purposes cited and yet young people themselves generally saw the intention behind exclusion as punishment. For example, exclusion blocked off access to an important social forum – school: 'My highest suspension has been ten days and I didn't like it because I was sitting in and I was bored and everybody else was at school' (S1 boy).

This view was endorsed by a second boy 'I have been suspended twice for five days each time. I got snibbed [locked-in] because I got suspended and it was pure boring because nobody was about' (S1 boy).

School staff tended not to construct exclusions as punishment but as a means of removing from the classroom community significant personal and social pressure on others. At the extreme, exclusions could ensure that adults and young people in the classroom no longer had to tolerate on a daily basis the threat and the experience of abusive and aggressive behaviour. For example, one disciplinary referral from a teacher described how an S3 boy, one of the case studies discussed further on, was asked to stand outside the classroom because of an outburst he had had. When the teacher came to speak to him he called him *a f***ing bastard, f***ing black jake, f***ing poof.*

The punitive effect of exclusion seemed to rely on parental cooperation in that young people who were confined to their homes during exclusion were more likely to experience the exclusion as a punishment. There were differences in the level of parental support schools expected in the event of exclusion, with some parents unable or unwilling to control how young people spent their time when out of school. Some pupils took the view that exclusion was a break from the pressure and routine of school. During interviews, when asked if they undertook schoolwork during the period of their exclusion, some pupils were scathing about the idea 'If you're excluded, you're excluded. There's no point getting excluded if you are going to be doing the work, know what I mean? An exclusion is to get out of school' (S3 boy). 'My ma always asks for work but

I never do it. I tell her I am going out to play or I will see her after' (S2 boy).

One or two pupils interviewed went further, claiming to have had some agency in their exclusion:

> I just don't like it [school]. I had just . . . I was off school for about six months or something and I had just come back like that. It was getting up in the morning, you know, you are like that, 'Aw, naw, man, do ah need to go to school?' And it just puts you in a bad mood and when you come you are just in a bad mood already so you just start annoying teachers and that and you start giving them lip.
>
> (S2 boy)

It is possible that there was some bravado in these claims. The boys interviewed did not portray themselves as ever having lost control and reacted in anger to teachers or other pupils. Rather, they represented themselves as always in control and always able to manoeuvre situations to their own advantage. One principal teacher (PT) interviewed disputed the idea that some children set out to engineer their own exclusion:

> There is a myth that some children, just to get a break from school will try to get excluded. It is not my impression here that pupils go out to set up a situation that may lead to their exclusion. They may lack self-control or a situation may escalate but it is very rare that a child will provoke exclusion.
>
> (PT)

This view was endorsed by an assistant headteacher (AHT) from another LA 'Like people saying that some children laugh at exclusion, I have yet to hear, to see, a child that is happy to be excluded. I genuinely mean that' (AHT).

The existence of an Appeals system in relation to exclusion is one of the clearest indications that exclusions operate as a form of punishment – appeals are not needed against welfare-based approaches. A senior LA representative confirmed that school-based challenges to the decision to exclude a pupil rarely developed into formal appeals. This is consistent with the national pattern. In the 2003/04 session, there were just 26 appeals in 38,919 exclusions (SEED, 2005). In her own LA, the official attributed the low level of appeals to two reasons. First, the LA made the exclusion process as fair and as transparent as possible and, second, the appeals procedure was so slow that, by the time the appeal was heard, the exclusion period was over and the best that could happen was that the note of the exclusion would be expunged from the pupil's record. A central government policy officer concurred with this view. Appeals would always be after the event and he believed that parents generally saw no point in appealing in retrospect. The exclusion would have served the school's purpose(s) by the time any appeal was heard. The government official indicated that the low number of appeals was a concern. The systems supporting appeals were not responsive enough to prevent the exclusion taking place. On an alternative system of appeals, the LA representative said:

> That's a difficult one. I do not quite know how to resolve it because . . . we would almost have to have a system that enabled a parent to register an appeal on the day of the exclusion and where the appeal was heard within two or three days.
>
> (Senior education officer)

Lack of responsiveness in the system may not be the only reason why there were so few appeals. An AHT interviewed attributed the low level of appeals (he had none in his experience) to a certain feeling of powerlessness on the part of parents:

> A lot of our parents will rant and rave and say they are going to (Council HQ) to complain about the system and so on . . . they get a note with the exclusion telling them how to appeal but very few actually do . . . . In some respects, some of our parents do not stand up for themselves.
>
> (AHT)

With regard to appeals, there was evidence that parents' engagement with the school system did not empower them to challenge exclusions, even when they were informed about the formal mechanism. Occasions were noted where local community law centres offered support to parents seeking to challenge exclusion. The LA representatives saw the role of law centres in this respect as unhelpful but such criticisms could be construed as professional protectionism. While the 'rights' approach upheld by law centres forced a legalistic and procedurally orientated approach to exclusions, limiting the scope for professional 'welfare' interventions, it also enabled some parents to 'stand up for themselves'. The law centre approach challenged schools' supremacy in making decisions about children but the empowerment it offered to parents could still leave them ill-equipped for constructive participation in their children's education.

Findings from other studies endorse the view that pupils experience exclusion as a punishment. McCluskey (2008) notes that although policy guidelines on exclusion in Scotland (SEED, 2003), do not construct exclusion from school as a punishment, that is exactly how exclusion is perceived by pupils. Exclusion has been viewed as contributing to the vilification of young people and their families (Parsons, 2005). Commentators (Garland, 2001; Parsons, 2005; Matthews, 2005) have written about the impetus towards punishment, not just in schools, and have related this to political and cultural norms. Parsons (2005: 23) applies this analysis to responses to student disaffection in schools. He refers to the three discourses of social inclusion developed by Levitas and finds a strong element of MUD (moral underclass discourse) in how certain groups of pupils are treated. Challenging behaviour may be seen either as deserving of support or as meriting a punitive response:

> Part of the experience of disruptive behaviour among young people in school, is that they are hugely and publicly vilified, so are their parents and family, and so also are those who support them (especially if successful), and the negative consequences can be quite severe.
>
> (Parsons, 2005: 198)

Among those consequences are alienation from schooling, perhaps even from education as a lifelong pursuit.

Effects of exclusion on excluded young people

Pupils themselves have been reported as seeing exclusion as having punitive consequences into the future (McCluskey, 2008: 452). The discontinuity in education caused by exclusion could be one from which young people never recovered. And yet, education officials interviewed conveyed that exclusions were not intended to be punitive. This 'welfare' construction of exclusions required that they did not undermine the education of pupils. To that end in 2003, the guidelines on school exclusions (SEED, 2003) were amended to establish that exclusion from school should not be exclusion from education – the service would continue albeit in the home setting. The LA representatives strongly endorsed the position that schools were expected to provide homework packages for the period of the exclusion. However, it was acknowledged that there was as yet no established system to implement and monitor that aspect of exclusion guidelines within the LA. Within schools, there was much less support for the idea of homework packages, with some respondents indicating their view that it was unworkable:

> I think it is a piece of nonsense this – work will be provided. What do you do about their science? . . . I am sure there is some human rights legislation behind it but if teachers have limited preparation time, how do they go about doing it?
>
> (AHT)

Where excluded pupils saw exclusion as a break from schooling, they were likely to resist doing schoolwork during that period. Staff in schools setting the 'work' required by exclusion guidelines, were coming to see this as a token exercise designed to ensure compliance with legislation, rather than as an attempt to ensure continuity in the young person's education.

There was concern, too, from SEED that access to services (e.g. of therapists) normally gained through the school, would be closed off during the period of the exclusion. Pupils with Records of Needs were disproportionately represented in exclusion statistics, and concern for their welfare was reflected in LA guidelines to schools: 'In the case where the Authority considers that exclusion from the particular school is necessary, it is essential that the Authority take all reasonable steps to ensure that alternative provision for the pupil's special educational needs is made available' (LA 3). But right of access to services during the exclusion may not be taken up if and when pupils and their parents experience exclusion from school as a break from a demanding routine.

Also of concern is the number of children for whom exclusion from school resulted in exclusion from education in the long term. Sometimes, a 20-day exclusion would be accompanied by the recommendation (supported by the Director of Education) that a new placement in mainstream be found for the pupil. A new school would be asked to accept the pupil but parents then had to cooperate in enrolling their child in the new school:

> If the parents simply do not cooperate with that then you then have the youngsters in a limbo as we have – at least one – I think we have only one just now who, technically, should have been going to another school round about August (i.e. six months previously). His mother has not done so and he has been roaming the streets since then.
>
> (PT)

Pupils remained on the rolls of the original school until they had re-enrolled elsewhere and the school would then record their non-attendance as unauthorised absence. For families, the difficulty and the expense of maintaining a child at a school in another part of the city might be strong disincentives to keeping that child in school.

Differential impact of exclusions

Exclusions were experienced by families as well as by those young people immediately affected but, depending on how families were positioned, the impact of exclusion could be very different. Some professionals interviewed argued that exclusion could be constructive in that it prompted all those concerned to take time to review what had happened leading to the exclusion and enabled changes to be made. 'None of this should be about hurting or damaging. It should be about changing' (AHT).

This school had a number of placing requests and served a socially mixed community. Similarly, the headteacher of the school serving the most uniformly middle-class area explained that the school could rely on the prompt and explicit support of parents should any difficulty arise. Exclusion was occasionally needed to find out if there were other, deeper reasons for the pupils' behaviour. Then more appropriate support systems could be put in place. Exclusions, therefore, were not the end point in a hierarchy of sanctions but the means of providing a broad forum for planning the future support of the pupil. This school served a middle-class locality and enjoyed the support of an affluent and educationally active parent community. This school was over-subscribed, rejecting each year between 150 and 200 applications and, linked to this, the school had very few exclusions, so few that the statistical patterns and trends could not be gauged. Parents, although most of them were working, were easily contactable and highly responsive to school requests.

This was in stark contrast to the situation for schools in other parts of the same city. Schools in the LA with high rates of social exclusion reported great difficulty in involving parents in preventative measures and in securing their support once the decision to exclude had been taken. Sometimes the reasons were material:

> A lot of parents either do not have a phone or the number keeps on changing or they have not bought their card for the mobile phone . . . because our parents are so poor, I am talking about a lot just now, they have a mobile phone in the house – there is no land line. It seems to them to be cheaper because you have not got a big bill coming in at the end . . . .
> (AHT)

Exclusions always sent a signal to families but, for parents with fewer economic and cultural resources, not necessarily one to which they could respond as the school would like. Commentators (Munn *et al.* 1997; Munn *et al.* 2000; McDonald and Thomas, 2003) have written of the personal impact of school exclusion on pupils and their families. In these studies, parents were reported as experiencing a strong sense of powerlessness and hurt as a result of their child's exclusion. McDonald and Thomas (2003) found that negative experiences of school were intensified when the parents concerned were those of pupils who were excluded. Exclusion impacted on families' longer-term engagement with school, further alienating them from an important mainstream service. Hegemonic discourses about parenting dominate teacher attitudes and these emphasise the rights and the duties of parents. Vincent (2000: 131) comments: 'The exercise of the right to involvement and the fulfilment of that duty to be involved is clearly easier for some parents than others'.

Parents' engagement with schooling was crucial in determining if the processes leading to exclusion were supportive of the interests of the pupil or were merely punitive. More broadly, social class influenced experience of exclusions with exclusions compounding the sense of powerlessness felt by some families. Parents of excluded pupils could feel particularly unable to influence dominant discourses of the school and could themselves experience exclusion from school processes of decision-making (MacDonald and Thomas, 2003). Vincent (2000) argues that even parent-centred organisations serve as channels for the dissemination of hegemonic discourses about parenting. The misrecognition of some parents is underpinned by economic factors, by all of the ways in which low income restricts family life – poor housing, inadequate diet, health problems, limited access to the means of communication, inability to participate in local and community life.

Consistency and fairness

Exclusions were not generally applied in ways which were in proportion to the related incidents. A strict tariff system where particular types of incidents attracted a set period of exclusion was rejected by all of the school-based staff interviewed. Government guidelines (SEED, 2003) were not prescriptive in that sense. They left considerable scope for local authorities and schools to take into account factors other than the incident itself. Some local authorities, however, had stipulated a fixed penalty for certain offences such as association with drugs, use of alcohol and for violence. In the view of several participants, the stipulation was upheld rigidly for drugs but much less so for alcohol and for violence, where other information was regularly used to qualify decisions about exclusions. One PT pointed out that the automatic application of an exclusion tariff for violence was very difficult where 'violence' was so open to interpretation:

> That's an area in which, although that is the headteacher's stated policy, it is frequently breached, and if we were to operate it in a literal sense, where every punch thrown or every kick led to an exclusion, it would in actual fact be unworkable. I would have to say that the interpretation of that, the whole violence rule, does cause me some concerns. We have put out pupils who have not come back.... other pupils have carried out similar activities and they have been excluded for either very short periods or indeed dealt with through the Assistant Heads.
>
> (PT)

Thus, flexibility to apply exclusions in the light of wider knowledge of the pupil and the circumstances can lead to inconsistency and unfairness. A senior education officer from a large LA was aware of inconsistencies in the use of exclusions but thought it important to maintain the flexibility allowed to schools in determining the appropriateness of exclusions. She argued that, in balancing consistency against flexibility, the weighting should go to giving schools flexibility because 'what worked very well for some young people did nothing for others' (Senior Education Officer).

For the young people interviewed, fairness was a central concern. Often, they could see some basis to decisions about the length of an exclusion:

JK: What are different spells of exclusion? What's the reason for that?
S2 PUPIL: Cause it's what you do. There's stuff you do. But if you get an exclusion for whatever ... having hundreds of punnies.... that's not very bad, is it?

But you get three days. But that time I got accused of hitting a teacher with a stone, know what I mean, that's how I got twenty days. That was, like, dodgy, know what I mean?

Sometimes, though, it was felt not only that different schools applied different criteria in exclusions (see later on) but also that, even within the same school, pupils were treated differently. This might be related to gender but, importantly for pupils, it was perceived to be a function of teachers' expectations of different pupils. The boys interviewed felt that they had been negatively labelled and had suffered discriminatory treatment as a consequence:

See the day in Craft and Design, a stink bomb got set off, right, and I don't know but I think the teacher thinks it's me because I'm the worst, one of the bad people in the class, but it wasn't me. . . . see like somebody that's good behaved? He would never blame them even if it was.

(S2 pupil)

The young people interviewed endorsed the view of one PT that schools were very sensitive to their image and that incidents which were in themselves minor might attract exclusion because the incident was seen to be damaging to the school's reputation: 'Those youngsters who bring the school into disrepute, for example, by misbehaving during an outside speaker's presentation, will almost automatically be excluded, even if the actual incident was a relatively minor one' (PT, LA 1). The sensitivity of schools in this respect is a result of their need to exist in a market context where placing requests in and out of schools were influential in assuring the future of the school.

Munn et al. (1997) revealed that exclusion generated mutual distrust between home and school. All pupils in that study indicated that their exclusion had made their parents angry and there were examples of parents or staff feeling that they had been let down or betrayed by some statement or apparent non-cooperation on the part of the other (Munn et al. 1997: 6). A key issue for excluded pupils and their families in these studies was the fairness or otherwise of the exclusion: 'Pupils were conscious that they got labeled as troublemakers and as a consequence got picked on. Pupils who came from the "wrong part of town" perceived teachers as more likely to pick on them for that reason' (Munn et al. 1997: 5).

Also contributing to pupils' perceptions of unfairness was the belief that they were judged according to the behaviour of older siblings (Munn et al. 2000).

Effectiveness

What purposes were served by exclusions? In common with other studies (McCluskey, 2008), pupils here saw exclusion as an ineffective means of maintaining order in schools, although in the short term, some excluded pupils conceded that exclusions might create welcome respite for teachers. Pupils' views of the effectiveness of exclusions were shared by many professional participants. Particularly questionable, in the view of some of the professional key informants was whether exclusions were effective in deterring disruptive behaviour in future. The policy officials interviewed, in contrast, cited the deterrent function of exclusion as one of only two purposes they served, although they emphasised that the use of exclusion as a deterrent should always be as a last resort. The other purpose, in the official view, was to protect the learning and teaching of the majority of pupils. This purpose is discussed further later on. In arguing against the deterrent effect of exclusions, school-based professionals made the point that schools had only limited control over some of the factors which led to exclusion. Sometimes, in spite of the development of internal anti-exclusion strategies, exclusions might increase significantly because of events outwith the school. One AHT from a secondary school spoke of an increase in gang warfare as a result of a tragic accident when an 11-year-old boy had been killed on the nearby motorway while being chased during territorial fighting. Reprisals had been going on and had involved a number of boys at the school, resulting in their exclusion.

There was some agreement that exclusion sent out a signal to the local community that certain kinds of behaviour, for example, violent behaviour or behaviour related to the use of drugs or alcohol, were unacceptable to the school. Exclusion for these kinds of behaviours might be seen to signal the school's position but the prime audience was not the excluded pupil or his family but other members of the school and the wider community:

> it is probably . . . effective in cases where there has been a fight, violence of that sort, the parent of the aggrieved child will hear that his or her assailant was excluded and will get a sense of satisfaction that the school takes the concern seriously.
>
> (PT)

Exclusions here were not viewed as effective in curtailing the behaviour which was dangerous to the young person and to others. LA representatives concurred with the view that exclusions drew a line in the sand with regard to certain kinds of behaviour, indicating that, although centrally funded initiatives had made a significant impact in reducing the number of exclusions overall, there were still a number of drugs and violence-related incidents for which exclusion was considered an appropriate response. As previously noted, very few exclusions are for incidents or behaviours of that kind.

Exclusion as a means of protecting learning and teaching was the second of two purposes cited by government representatives and it was the only purpose where exclusions were seen to have some effect. There was agreement that exclusion served the interests of others in affording them some peace and possibly protection: '... it is effective in that it does make life easier for other children, it does make life easier for teachers' (PT).

School-based professionals were clear that exclusion prevented interruption of teaching and learning, an understandable advantage in a political climate where results were used to judge the effectiveness of teachers and schools. School staff did not argue that there were commensurate benefits for the young people who were excluded. The effectiveness of exclusions was seen to rest entirely upon the benefits they brought to the school community as a whole. LA officials recognised that the possibility of exclusion could remove the need for schools to develop more inclusive practices: 'I am not saying it is an easy exit for children because the other side of the coin is to ensure that schools are developing more in-house strategies, more effective learning and teaching, more appropriate curriculum models' (Education officer).

There was unanimity among professionals that the broader social context of the school constituted the significant factor in exclusion rates. An AHT from a school serving a very disadvantaged area commented:

> You get a lot of poor souls down at [Council HQ] ... For all sorts of reasons, school, education, social work, whoever, has not managed to give them and their families the necessary support. At the end of the day, we have got to run the school for the other seven hundred kids in here.
> (AHT, secondary school)

The reference here to 'the other seven hundred kids' was echoed elsewhere in the data in comments from professional participants. Exclusions were most strongly justified in official and professional accounts as a means of protecting the interests of those not excluded. 'Others' were usually conveyed as the hard-working and motivated majority of pupils. Pupils themselves, whether or not they had been excluded, had no sense of this binary in the pupil population. While most pupils in Scottish schools never experience exclusion, neither do they see themselves as distinct from those who have been excluded. Similarly, McCluskey (2008), in her study of pupils' views of exclusion, found no basis there for the commonly held distinction between disruptive and disrupted pupils. Throughout the key informant interviews, the clearest differences in perspectives on exclusions were those between professionals and pupils, not least in how far these two groups highlighted difference within the pupil population.

Conclusion

This chapter has explored the meanings of school exclusions against a policy background of social inclusion. Social inequalities were seen to influence school exclusions with social class coming through as a strong factor differentiating pupils and the likelihood of their exclusion. Insights were offered as to how the agency of middle-class parents might forestall the exclusion of their sons and daughters. Schools enjoyed flexibility in judging the penalty for a particular offence but this caused pupils especially to see exclusions as unfairly administered.

School exclusions were noted as serving a range of purposes. The official view was that some of these purposes served excluded pupils, for example, in deterring them from future wrongdoing. Statistics revealed that some 20 per cent of excluded pupils had been repeatedly excluded and there was some scepticism among school-based key informants as to the deterrent value of exclusions. The pointers were that the overriding purpose of exclusion was to benefit school staff and other pupils. This view is understandable where some pupils are undermining learning and teaching but it challenges policy constructions of education as inclusive. More than that, there is little possibility of schools functioning as sites where the transmission of social disadvantage might be broken. Exclusion, especially repeated exclusion, increases existing inequality by undermining excluded pupils' experience of schooling by alienating those pupils and their families from the education system.

The segregating effect of exclusions could be seen in the view that their primary purpose was the protection of learning and teaching for the majority. In the communication of this view, there emerged a sense of excluded pupils as unworthy of what schools had to offer, as different from the majority of deserving pupils. This distinction was made by professionals and did not come through from pupils themselves. In drawing a line between excluded pupils and the majority of pupils, moral judgements were apparent in comments made – the same judgements pervading 'moral underclass' constructions of social inclusion.

Chapters 4, 5 and 6 will use empirical data to consider how school exclusions relate to the social class and gender identities of excluded pupils. Before that, the next chapter will discuss the theoretical influences used in analysing data.

Chapter 3

Social class, gender and exclusions

Introduction

The meanings of school exclusion in a policy context have been considered. This chapter will now relate school exclusions to social class and gender identities. A theoretical framework will be established here prior to the analysis of data which follows in Chapters 4, 5 and 6. A main question pursued throughout these chapters concerns how the negotiation of gender and class identities in school settings has bearing upon exclusion from school. School-based studies have probed gender, and the intersections of class and gender, in the processes through which boys and girls negotiate identities in school settings (Skelton, 1997; Francis, 2000; 2005; Reay, 2001; 2002; Renold, 2004; Jackson, 2006a; 2006b). This body of work will be discussed here and used to query, first, why working-class boys are disproportionately excluded and, second, what the experience of excluded girls and boys can tell us about femininities and masculinities in school settings. Class cultural analyses of social class will be drawn upon to understand how class identities shape, and are shaped by, girls and boys' everyday experience of schooling. Less recent studies are also highly relevant for the discussion here, originating as they do in a period when the educational disadvantage of the working class was a main focus of enquiry for educational sociologists. Differences between those pupils who are excluded and other pupils are explored against a background of educational disadvantage and wider social inequality.

Social identities

Sociologists have long been concerned with the educational disadvantage of the working class and with the role played by schooling in social and cultural reproduction (Hargreaves, 1967; Willis, 1978; Ball, 1981). Researchers in the 1970s and the 1980s were particularly concerned with the sub-cultures of working-class boys/young men and with demonstrating how these distinct groupings arose from and re-inforced class solidarity and resistance. Oppositional behaviour in school settings arose from the impetus for working-class boys to develop the collective identity required for their future lives as workers under industrial capitalism. As working-class men, their need would be to stave off the worst encroachments of that system through a culture which encompassed both resistance and accommodation. 'Working class counter-school culture is the specific milieu in which a sense of manual labour power and an awareness of how to apply it to manual work is produced' (Willis, 1978: 2).

Alienation from schooling, leading to anti-school behaviour, was embedded in the processes of forming class and gender-based identities which were in turn located in larger processes reproducing patterns of inequality (Bynner *et al.* 1998: 4). This analysis of anti-school behaviour, the 'resistance' model, was persuasive but has been challenged by the virtual collapse of the youth labour market since the late 1970s. Gone are the days when cohorts of young men and young women moved *en masse* from school to local factories, mines or shipyards. The post-school transitions of young people are now individualised, risk-laden and protracted (Furlong and Cartmel, 2007). At the same time, concerns with the impact of wider social identities on schooling became politically unfashionable when school improvement orthodoxy came to dominate schools policy.

In the 1970s and the 1980s, identity politics came to the fore: recognition rather than re-distribution was a focus for political campaigning by a range of activists seeking equal rights. Gender displaced class as the main social category with both feminist political activism and gender theorising concerned exclusively with femininities. Phillips (1997) argued that the predominance of the Marxist or 'the materialist analysis' – with its emphasis on economic identity above all other forms of identity – had to be dislodged to enable proper consideration of the damaging impact of cultural and social constructions on particular groups – women, Blacks, homosexuals. Analyses which rested on social class alone would fail to account for, or even acknowledge, devastating forms of oppression and exploitation, for example, domestic violence and the abuse of children. Social inequality was not necessarily economic or material in nature. The oppression and exploitation experienced by women and by 'racial', sexual and other minorities took the form of cultural domination, non-recognition and disrespect (Young, 1990; Phillips, 1997; Fraser, 1997). The processes of reproducing inequalities relating to class, gender ethnicity, sexuality were seen to be tied up with the formation of social identities (Haywood and Mac an Ghaill, 2006).

The relationship between various dimensions of identity has been contentious. Early gender theorising failed to offer an analysis of how gender related to other forms of social identity, especially to social class, while feminine experience was neglected, and/or assumed to be a reflection of male experience (McRobbie, 1980; Skeggs, 1992; Rattansi and Pheonix, 1997), in, for example, studies of youth sub-cultures in the 1970s and the 1980s. For feminists, constructions of social class were male-orientated, rigid and trapped in a working-class/middle-class binary. The omission of class analyses from identity theorising, however, resulted in the normalising of middle-class experience and, in analyses of schooling, a failure to engage with the single most important source of inequality of outcomes. Identities of class, race and gender were seen to be unitary and stable but, at least in the theorising of identities, this view has been substantially revised. Across the social sciences, there has been a re-thinking of the nature of identities and of the relationship between the individual and the social world in identity construction. Rattansi and Pheonix (1997) offer one account of this, delineating six aspects in the development of identity theorising.

1 Identities are relational. Any particular identity only has meaning in relation to difference, that is, in contrast to what it is not;
2 Identities are not located in the 'essence' of a person. Rather, they are produced in specific social contexts which 'normalise' some forms of identity and stigmatise others;
3 Individuals occupy multiple positions and therefore have a range of identities with different ones acquiring salience in different contexts;
4 Identities are always in process, conditioned by and within specific social contexts;
5 Identities are shaped by the unconscious as well as the conscious self, which is neither in complete control nor in possession of complete self-knowledge;
6 Social and cultural formations are themselves shifting and contribute to the openness and provisionality of identities (Rattansi and Pheonix, 1997: 127).

More complex theorising of identities has supported school-based research analysing the processes through which multiple and fluid identities are negotiated and re-negotiated in specific contexts, contributing to the reproduction of inequalities.

In a policy arena, superficial analyses using gender alone, unmediated by other forms of identity, have been criticised. Boys and their achievements in schools, it is argued, should be seen as multiply constructed within the intersections of a variety of social positions, including issues of race, class, sexuality and ethnicity (Frank *et al.* 2003: 123). Archer and Yamashita (2003) coin the term *'culturally entangled masculinities'* and argue that there is evidence of the 'normalisation' of particular, white, middle-class values within education which encompass 'laddishness' but fail to grasp the extent to which some boys experience strong emotional attachment to identities grounded outside of the education context (Archer and Yamashita, 2003: 129). Official responses to boys' under-attainment in the UK and elsewhere have most often been rooted in a highly simplified view of gender, leading to misrepresentations of patterns of pupil achievement and lending weight to the criticism that identities are so enmeshed that to separate out and study one form only, such as gender, leads to distortions and misunderstandings. While acknowledging the risks in focusing on particular strands of identity and ignoring others such as ethnicity, disability and religion, this book will do just that. In focusing upon social class and gender identities here, the intention is not to deny the salience of other aspects of identity.

Masculinities and femininities

Feminist concerns and efforts in the 1970s were directed towards changing the unequal position of women in society, leading to the achievement of landmark UK legislation in the Sex Discrimination Act (1976) and the Equal Opportunities Act (1976). Long-standing stereotyped views of women as having primary roles as wives and mothers were seen as having shaped the experience of girls in school systems (Spender, 1982; Walkerdine, 1989). Riddell (2000) notes that both national advice and local authority policy in Scotland, although identifying gender factors in, for example, patterns of subject uptake, did not problematise these findings in relation to school practices. It was instead left to teachers' organisations, including the National Union of Teachers (NUT), the Educational Institute of Scotland (EIS), and the General Teaching Council (GTC), established in Scotland in 1965, to point out implications, for example, in curriculum choices which limited girls' views of themselves and their futures. In the 1970s, 'equal opportunities' in schools was a grass-roots issue with progress being driven by activist teachers, contrasting with the managerialist ethic soon to stifle the broader professional commitments of the teaching profession. In a pamphlet to its members intended as 'a positive assertion against sexism' the EIS criticised the situation in classrooms of the time where:

- boys demand and receive a generous share of teacher time;
- boys receive a disproportionate share of hands-on experience (e.g. in science or computing);
- boys receive apologies from teachers when asked to undertake non-traditional tasks;
- boys are rewarded for being assertive;
- boys are advised not to act like girls; and
- boys receive a disproportionate share of coveted class materials.
(EIS, 1989: para. 3.2.5, p. 5: cited in Riddell, 2000: 41)

In recent research reminiscent of the message conveyed by the EIS 16 years earlier, Francis (2005) records girls' experience in classrooms:

> The tendencies for girls to seat themselves on the peripheries of the classroom compounds the impression of girls as pushed to the margins of mixed-sex school life. Boys' physical domination of the classroom and playground space has been well documented. In the classroom, boys simply tend to take up more space than do girls. Even when sitting at desks boys

tend to sprawl more and take up more room, and when moving around the classroom their activities are more invasive of space.

(Francis, 2005: 12–13)

Even though the position of girls within schooling seemed to be unchanged, at least in some respects, concerns shifted to boys who appeared to be faring less well than girls in examination systems. Understandings of masculinities were developed by a range of theorists, for example, Mac an Ghaill (1994), Epstein (1997 and 1998), Connell (1995 and 2002), Skelton (1997). Jackson (2002: 39) identified four main strands in this development:

- masculine identities are historically and culturally situated
- multiple masculinities exist
- there are dominant and subordinate forms of masculinity
- masculinities are actively constructed in school settings.

Of particular value in the theorising of masculinities has been the theory of hegemonic masculinities (Connell, 1995; 2002), based on the structure of gender/sexual power relations. Connell argued that there was gender politics within masculinities; that men seek to develop relations of alliance, subordination and domination within any group of men, and do so in an ongoing way through everyday interactions (Connell, 1995: 37). This theory has been particularly useful in understanding how a range of masculinities are negotiated and re-negotiated in school settings (Skelton, 2001; Francis, 2000; Renold, 2004). Schools are not merely a neutral background against which gender and other power relations are negotiated. Instead, schools act as institutional agents in gender-forming processes, endorsing particular forms of femininity and masculinity and are involved in negotiating the power relations between them (Connell, 1989). Within that power structure, boys define themselves as 'Subject' against the 'Other' (Paechter, 1998). Any association with femininity is located within the 'Other', including masculinities which do not conform to the hegemonic standard of what it is to be a 'real' man (Kenway and Fitzclarence, 1997: 119–20).

Socially and sometimes physically marginalised in classrooms, playgrounds and so on, boys unable or unwilling to negotiate high-status masculinities might experience harassment and bullying from boys within or aspiring to the hegemony (Mac an Ghaill, 1994; Connell, 1995; Renold, 2004). Processes of excluding and disrespecting some boys and all girls are the same processes by which the 'culturally exalted status' (Renold, 2004: 250) of hegemonic masculinities might be achieved. On the other hand, boys seeking to achieve and maintain hegemonic identities also experience difficulties (Renold, 2004: 249). For boys who were excluded from secondary school in this study, the behaviour leading to their exclusion could be viewed as conscious attempts to attain or consolidate high status with their peer group. Schools also confer and withhold status, and in primary schools seemed to do so in ways which were acceptable to boys and girls. Questions are raised further on as to why some secondary-school boys and girls opted out of school-led processes of recognition and validation, especially for academic achievement.

The study of gender, and masculinities, within a complex system of power relations has been helpful in analysing 'problem' masculinities, such as violent behaviour. Commentators have pointed to the over-representation of men in statistics for crime, particularly for violent crime (Connell, 2002; Mills, 2001). These concerns with masculinities and violence extended into education and became particularly pointed after the murders at Columbine High School in the US in 1999 when two boys shot dead twelve students and one teacher in their own school. Mills (2001: 2) examines the ways in which violence has become associated with 'normalised' forms of masculinity. Sex-based harassment of girls by boys and of boys by other boys is often a form of 'boundary policing' which serves both to normalise particular constructions of masculinity and to re-inforce a boy's positioning within an hierarchy of masculinities (Mills, 2001: 2). Connell argues that 'problem' masculinities such as violent behaviour can be understood as part of diversity in gender practices and consciousness (Connell, 1995: 249). By this account, some 'problem' masculinities at least, arise from a false consciousness of masculinities and the structures of power relations, with the remedy lying in the re-education of men (Mills, 2001; Martino and Pallotta-Chiarolli, 2003). The behaviour of boys in this study was less extreme than the examples cited here but boys frequently reported violence as a feature of their lives and some of their exclusions were a result of physical assaults and fighting. Approaches to challenging violence in schools rely upon disrupting the association between violence and dominant masculinities, by encouraging pupils to query how high-status masculinities have acquired their status, and by asking whose interests are served anyway by allocating such status to those particular masculinities (Mills, 2001: 20).

So what happened to girls in the 1990s as masculinities became the focus for so much theorising? They seemed again to have become invisible as a focus on outcomes for one group (boys) distorted perceptions of the performance of other groups (Blyth and Milner, 1996; Plummer, 2000). The focus on boys' attainment in the 1990s had resulted in misinterpretation of girls' performance within overall patterns of school attainment. There was evidence that groups other than boys were faring badly; the significant achievement of middle-class girls had been widely misinterpreted as indicative of a rise in the achievement of all girls (Plummer, 2000). As a result of the focus on boys, particularly of perceptions that their behaviour was so much worse than girls, there had been less investigation of girls' experience. Research has been less concerned to analyse the processes, in-school and out-of-school, by which girls negotiate their multiple identities. Occasionally, 'problem' girls in school settings were portrayed as passive and introverted, as victims even. This view of girls was in marked contrast to Connell's portrayal of boys as exercising agency in the negotiation of their masculinities. While acknowledging that girls' challenging behaviour took different forms, there were indications that feminine 'problem' behaviour was less likely to lead to exclusion because, for example, girls adopted stereotypical female responses, such as crying, thereby avoiding exclusion. Osler et al. (2002: 48) describe the reaction of some girls in school settings when confronted with a charge of wrongdoing: 'the adoption of a remorseful stance, crying and the use of verbal skills including denial, excuses and apologies were strategies used by many girls to manoeuvre around school disciplinary procedures'.

Similarly, there were concerns that the behaviour of girls, while less likely to be of the very challenging kind that leads to exclusion, could be highly problematic and just as indicative of disaffection with schooling as the 'acting out' behaviour of boys. Osler et al. (2002) note that girls' exclusion from school was much more likely to be self-exclusion in the form of truancy or other disengagement from school and classroom processes. McLaughlin (2005: 54), exploring the psychosocial experience of 'problem' girls and alluding to the work of Brown and Gilligan (1992), reports that adolescent girls seemed to experience a 'loss of voice' at that stage, losing the 'ordinary courage' to speak their minds. This 'loss of voice' is linked to the social construction of gender (McLaughlin, 2005). Other writers (Osler and Vincent, 2003), too, have commented upon the link between girls' relationships, agency and experience of school. Their focus has been on girls who fare badly in school settings and whose behaviour is characterised by passivity and withdrawal, very different from the problem behaviour likely to lead to formal exclusion. Girls constitute just 20 per cent of school exclusions but there are indications that the behaviour of these excluded girls is becoming more prevalent among girls generally with the rise of a 'ladette' culture documented, and usually deplored, in some sections of the media. Jackson (2006a; 2006b), in outlining secondary pupils' and teachers' perceptions, described ladettes as girls/young women who 'act hard, smoke, swear, fight occasionally, drink, disrupt lessons, are cheeky and/or rude to teachers, are open about (heterosexual) sex, and are loud or "gobby"' (Jackson, 2006a: 346).

Jackson differentiates between tomboys and ladettes, characterising ladettes as setting out to be attractive to boys. Even when wearing tomboyish clothes, ladettes would take care that some aspect of their appearance was overtly heterosexualised. The teachers in Jackson's study reported that challenging behaviour among girls appeared to be increasing. Official statistics offer further evidence that this is the case. Since 1971, Scotland's youth justice system has included a Children's Hearings System which provides *a structure of intervention and support for children who are considered to require compulsory measure of care and/or control* (Munn et al. 2000: 173). Referrals of girls to the Reporter to Children's Hearings have increased substantially over the past five years from 3,000 in 2000/01 to 4,200 in 2005/06. In addition, recent statistics on school exclusions in Scotland (Scottish Government, 2007) show a tenfold increase in the number of girls excluded from primary schools in the 2005/06 session, although the number of girls excluded remained small in comparison with the number of boys. These indications from statistics have been seized upon by the press as indicative of a rise in 'ladette' culture among young women with a leading Scottish daily newspaper commenting that the difference between masculinity and femininity was starting to disappear (*The Herald*, 18/9/2006).

An alternative view is that a wider range of femininities is coming to the fore, with girls and women able to challenge stereotypical views of what it is to be feminine, and to 'do' femininities in public spaces. Neither masculinity nor femininity is monolithic. Gender commentators frequently refer to a range of masculinities and femininities but pluralities have led to typologies of masculinities and femininities, often utilising the concept of hegemonic masculinities (Connell, 1995; Reay, 2001). Francis (2000: 13) is critical of 'types' of masculinity and femininity for two reasons. First, she argues that this tends to reify gender and misrepresents how fluid gender identities can be. Gender is not as fixed as 'typing' implies, although she accepts that it is sometimes helpful in illustrating how, for example, boys in school settings construct masculinity in different ways. Her second objection to 'types' of masculinity and femininity is more conceptual; if there are different kinds of masculinities and femininities, what do masculinities have in common with each other and what do femininities have in common with each other? For example, some 'types' of feminine behaviour, such as those leading to girls' exclusion from school, might be very like some 'types' of masculine behaviour, might even be described as masculine, as they have been in the newspaper quotation mentioned earlier. Francis argues for a gender dichotomy with one (notional) masculinity and one (notional) femininity – oppositional to one another, shifting and flexible. Men and women who display traits assigned to the opposite sex can be accommodated within this conceptualisation of gender, that is, women can display masculine traits without themselves being considered masculine (Francis, 2000: 16). Gender formation processes encompass the negotiation of a number of femininities but Francis (2005) and Reay (2001: 164) note that, although there are multiple femininities, what they all have in common is their deferment of power to the boys. 'Within both localised and dominant discourses being a boy was still seen as best by all the boys and by a significant number of girls' (Reay, 2001: 164).

'Ladette' behaviour also raises questions about the relationship of gendered behaviour to social class. Jackson comments that, although ladettes are transgressing gender boundaries in their behaviour, their confirmed heterosexual attitudes mean they cause no disruption to the gender order (Jackson, 2006a: 354). Does ladette behaviour map on to views of working-class women? There is no evidence that ladette behaviour is confined to working-class girls but its characterisation in the press may relate to a broader and long-established view of working-class women as less than respectable (Skeggs, 1997: 3). Of the 20 case studies of excluded pupils discussed in the chapters which follow, just three were girls (roughly reflecting the gender balance of exclusion statistics). Girls were excluded less often, for shorter periods of time and for less serious misdemeanours than boys. Some evidence emerged that girls' challenging behaviour related to economic factors, for example, to the stress caused by poverty, but also to their negotiation of particular working class and feminine identities in their relationships with school staff, male and female friends and their peer group more generally. Their challenging behaviour and exclusion from school can be related to their negotiation of class cultural and gender identities in school settings.

A main focus for this book is the intersection of gender with social class identities. Connell argued that there is a class politics within masculinity, noting that the privileged position enjoyed by men in the structure of gender power relations was compounded and enhanced for some men by class, race and generational differences (Connell, 1995: 249). Economic privilege, as well as gender privilege, structured power relations, so, for example, the hegemonies of working-class men in traditional sites such as factories were clearly less powerful than those masculine hegemonies operating in the US Pentagon (Connell, 1995: 76). What is the relationship between social class and gender identities? Femininities and masculinities are complex, shifting, layered and negotiated in school settings. A number of school-based studies trace these shifting patterns of 'identity work' (Reay, 2001; Renold, 2004) but for girls and boys engaged in it, there are limits to the permutations possible. 'Fixing' mechanisms limit the fluidity of identity construction (Reay, 2002). Gender identities can be negotiated within a limited span influenced by other aspects of identity, principally, it will be argued here, by social class.

Social class

Over three decades from the 1970s, social theorists debated the prioritising of one form of identity over others. The Marxist analysis which privileged economic or social class identity was seen to marginalise other forms of identity (Phillips, 1997), namely, cultural identities arising from, for example, gender, sexuality and ethnicity. Bourdieu (1990) had proposed that capital had forms other than the material, but, like wealth, these were susceptible to the politics of redistribution. From this broad conception came theories of social justice (Young, 1990; Fraser, 1997) which articulated the pursuit of a just society as encompassing the proper recognition of social groups previously experiencing discrimination, oppression or exploitation; as well as the redistribution of wealth. While the conceptualisation of social justice as plural has been influential in policy, significant disagreements have remained about the nature of the relationship between economic and cultural forms of injustice. As the theoretical debates continued, social class slipped away from the educational policy arena. Expectations of a meritocracy were generated in the 1950s and the 1960s by the post-war settlement (Arnot, 2002: 3) but the link between social class and educational disadvantage persisted. Concern about this problem faded as the 1980s wore on but the new century saw the return of class. Lucey (2001) commented that while some attempted to celebrate the 'death of class' in the 1980s and the 1990s, the importance of class in determining educational experience had never declined (Lucey, 2001: 177).

Although the concept of masculine hegemonies has been helpful in understanding gendered patterns of schooling, it has had limited value in understanding masculinities and schooling because its social class dimension is undeveloped. Key issues relating to inequalities in educational outcomes, questions about which boys and which girls were faring badly in schooling, and why, have not been susceptible to analysis using this concept alone. An earlier ethnography, *Learning to Labour* (Willis, 1978), analysed the processes through which masculine, working-class identities were negotiated in a school setting. A group of 'lads' were tracked during their last two years at school and into the first six months of work. The power of collective action, of solidarity, of the need to be differentiated from controlling forces, led to little value being placed upon the individual and therefore on mental activity (Willis, 1978: 146). 'Mental work' was irrelevant to future lives as manual workers under industrial capitalism. Willis' explanation of collective alienation and disengagement from schooling is challenged in a context where the post-school transitions of all young people are noted as fragmentary, risk-laden and individualised (Giddens, 1990; Beck, 1992). Differentiations within this analysis with repect to social class and gender will be discussed further. Although underlying class relationships may be harder to detect in a collapsed youth labour market, Furlong and Cartmel (2007: 13) note that traditional sources of inequality remain intact.

Schools and social change

Policy relating to pupils' behaviour and exclusion from school was criticised in Chapter 2 for being overly influenced by the school improvement movement (SIM) and for failing to take sufficient account of pupil identities drawn from wider contexts. In advanced industrial societies, those wider contexts changed dramatically in the final few decades of the twentieth century. Implications for young people have been differently constructed using a range of metaphors to describe processes of transition (Evans and Furlong, 1997: 17). In the 1960s, school-leavers found their *niche* in one of three stratified transitions – higher education followed by a career, an apprenticeship or training followed by a career or direct entry to an unskilled or semi-skilled job. An extension of the functionalist perspective in the 1970s constructed transitions as more complex, referring to *bridges*, *routes* and *pathways* as unemployment and participation in post-compulsory education increased. In the 1980s, structuralist conceptualisation of youth transitions used the metaphor of a *trajectory* in social space (Bourdieu, 1990) where destinations were determined by structural factors such as class, race and gender, educational achievement and labour market conditions, with individual characteristics counting for little. In contrast, Ulrich Beck, in describing 'the risk society' (Beck, 1992), has argued that the traditional agencies of social reproduction, such as schools and extended and nuclear families, are no longer effective in channelling young people into pre-determined niches and levels of society (Evans and Furlong, 1997: 33). Rather, a multitude of possible choices has opened up with an increased level of risk to be *navigated* on an individual basis: 'an increasing fragmentation of opportunity and experience; the processes of youth are highly differentiated, reflecting and constructing social division in society in complex ways' (Evans and Furlong, 1997: 33).

The destinations of working-class school leavers have changed since Willis wrote of the lads' futures in industrial capitalism. Social and economic changes of the past 20 or 30 years have led to a heightened sense of risk and a greater individualisation of experience among young people (Furlong and Cartmel, 1997). Transitions are more complex and protracted for all young people but the levels of insecurity experienced are mediated by class-based factors such as educational attainment, and the impact of low school attainment is experienced years after the end of schooling (Howieson and Ianelli, 2008).

Changing patterns of employment and unemployment have impacted upon working-class men's traditional role in the home as patriarchal breadwinner. Reay says: 'against the backdrop of contemporary economic change and the hegemony of global capitalism, it is white, working-class young men who have the strongest sense that their masculinities are under siege, and this has consequences for their defensive practices' (Reay, 2002: 232).

Not necessarily a defensive practice, but perhaps a way of counteracting the impact of economic change and globalisation, is the strong affinity of working-class men to local identities. The identities of young people in this study were often very localised, with boys in particular demonstrating very strong attachments to their own communities. For most working-class young people, life could be lived entirely within their own neighbourhood (Ingram, 2009: 428). This narrowness of experience will have been exacerbated by a lack of employment opportunities since travel to work took young people into new spaces. Archer and Yamashita (2003) discuss how working-class boys articulated a sense of belonging to a place as constituting an important part of their identities. This linked to their need to feel safe, to be known and accepted. Nayak (2003), writing about how boys in the north-east of England constructed their identities in an industrial context much-changed since their fathers' and grandfathers' days, underlines the importance of football support as part of a 'curriculum of the body' used by 'the Real Geordies' to construct their white, working-class, masculine identities in the absence of a future of manual labour in heavy industry. Through support of the local football team the boys are able to construct their own identities and to differentiate finely those identities from other masculinities. For example, differentiations were not just between those men who supported the team and those men who did not. Nayak (2003: 155) found that 'the Real Geordies' located their identity in physically attending matches, shouting and singing during matches and drinking in pubs before and after. Anoraks, on the other hand, while still supporting the club, would watch matches on SKY television or in the pub. In ways such as these could school sub-culture continue to forge industrial masculinities in a post-industrial context:

> For these 'local lads', football fandom provided them with the routines, rituals and forms of embodied regulation familiar to an older world of manual labour. Significantly, the cultural re-imagining of Geordie masculinities reconfigures the relationship to production within the fields of leisure and consumption.
>
> (Nayak, 2003: 156)

Nayak concludes by arguing that the Real Geordies' strong association to place and culture indicate that traditions of masculinity are not easily dislodged from the lives of young men whatever global changes might imply. Neither do these boys inhabit 'dominant, hegemonic masculinities' for their claims to power were more precarious and contingent upon time, space and social context. Within schools, it may be possible to see boys as constructing identities against a background of social change not fully comprehended. The individualisation of their transitions to adult life contrasted with earlier generations, but their valuing of strong collective identities had not changed. In the workplace, collectivism had been a strategy for limiting the encroachments of industrial capitalism, generating a consciousness of, and a pride in, working-class identity. No longer expressed as class consciousness, boys' identities revealed strong group differentiations around football and locality.

Class cultural identities

Willis brought to the fore cultural as well as economic differentiations (Arnot, 2003; Connell, 2002). Gender theorists have attributed boys' antipathy towards academic work to the perception that to achieve in school, or at least to be seen to achieve in school, was associated with femininity, was 'uncool' and therefore challenging to the kinds of masculinities boys wished to pursue. For Willis' 'lads', the 'Otherness' of school work lay in its associations with middle-class futures, very different from how the 'lads' predicted their own working lives. Arnot's re-evaluation of *Learning to Labour* (Arnot, 2003) accords a measure of agency to the 'lads' in their resistance to school norms whereas commentators had previously criticised Willis' work because structure was seen to prevail entirely over agency, with the 'lads' trapped in a pre-determined working-class destiny. Questions about the agency of excluded pupils, and of schools, will arise in the following chapters when empirical data will be used to probe the processes leading to exclusion from school. That analysis will draw upon cultural conceptualisations of social class which have enabled the relationship between structure and agency to be re-framed.

Recent research into social class identities has used a cultural analysis of class, concerned with 'uncovering and exposing the unacknowledged normality of the middle classes . . . and its corollary, the equally unacknowledged pathologisation and diminishing of the working class' (Reay, 2006: 289).

These approaches utilise conceptual tools of habitus, capital and field (Bourdieu, 1990) to analyse how a range of identities is developed within social rules and structures. The concept of habitus, in particular, provides a method for empirical investigations by showing how inequalities are played out in everyday practices. Habitus explains how an individual thinks, feels and behaves as a result of early childhood experiences, principally of socialisation within the family (Reay, 1995; Arnot, 2002: 42). Although the habitus is capable of change over a lifetime, the effects of early training can never be fully reversed (Arnot, 2002: 43). An individual's habitus can be viewed *as a complex internalised core from which everyday experiences emanate* (Reay, 1995: 357). For sociologists, the appeal of the habitus is that it enables structure and agency to be considered together, allowing analysis of the relationship between the two. In individual experience, habitus and field interact in a continuing way, enabling studies utilising these concepts to capture the processes, or negotiations, between the individual and the context or field. Exclusions will be treated further on as a feature of the relationship between boys and girls and the context of their schools. While the habitus allows for individual agency, it also predisposes individuals to certain ways of behaving – 'identity work' takes place within a limited range of possibilities. For example, teachers in the case study schools discussed further on sometimes expressed frustration that some of their pupils did not have higher aspirations. For the boys and girls concerned, the possibilities envisaged by their teachers did not appear to exist.

Discussion here will also use the concept of capitals. Bourdieu delineated four types of capital – economic (wealth), cultural (encompassing language, appearance and educational background), social (membership of groups and social networks) and symbolic (that is associated with one's role, authority and prestige). Capital is the resources that people accumulate and exchange in order to maintain their positions of power within a field of society. Like economic capital, these resources are also capable of re-distribution. Each type of capital may present itself in concrete or material form, and its value at particular times is determined by the field or context in which it operates (Bourdieu and Wacquant, 1992: 98). The concepts of capital and habitus have been widely used to understand how engagement with, and advantage from, schooling varies considerably across education systems where statutory equality of access pertains. In studies of inequality in higher education (Ball *et al.* 2002; Noble and Davies, 2009) and of the inclusion of students with disabilities (DiGeorgio, 2009) the concepts of habitus and capital have enabled sophisticated analyses.

Some studies go further than acknowledging the intersections of different identities to assert social class as an underpinning, and not just a mediating, aspect of identity (Skeggs, 1997; Reay, 1998; Plummer, 2000; Reay and Wiliam, 1999). In a case study of Shaun and his experience in a London 'sink' secondary school, Reay (2002) shows how a working-class boy struggles, at some personal cost, to maintain his 'tough' status with his peer group while simultaneously aspiring to achieve at school. Shaun and his sisters live with their mother, a lone parent, in poverty, surviving on state benefits. Reay sees in Shaun's struggle an illustration of how gender and class identities interact: Shaun loves his entirely female family and shares their values but he recognises that life on the estate where he lives demands his conformity to aggressive forms of masculinity. His class identity shapes his gender identity, forcing him to construct his toughness as philanthropic, to be used in support of weaker peers and needy teachers. Working-class masculinity is shown to be 'more complex, nuanced and fragile' (Reay, 2002: 223) than has sometimes been portrayed within dominant discourses.

Embodied identities

How does habitus produce gendered as well as classed subjectivities? Bourdieu explains that:

> Because the classificatory schemes through which the body is apprehended and appreciated are always grounded twofold, both in the social division of labour and in the sexual division of labour, the relation to the body is specified according to sex and according to the form that the division of labour between the sexes takes depending on the position occupied in the social division of labour.
>
> (Bourdieu, 1990: 72)

In the family, children become aware of their mothers', and fathers' bodies at the same time as they develop awareness of the definition of the social functions of men and women, generating associations between male and female and the division of labour. The transmission of culture is closely tied in with its embodiment.

The girls and boys in the chapters which follow performed their identities in a number of ways, for example, through their physical bearing; their clothes; and, most strikingly, their speech. The notion of culture as embodied is a key element in Bourdieu's theory on which he places considerable emphasis. The embodiment of the habitus is not about how the body is represented to itself or by itself – representation implies some space between the individual and the body and a level of consciousness – rather 'What is "learned by body" is not something that one has like knowledge that can be brandished, but something that one is' (Bourdieu, 1990: 73).

Habitus is not to be located merely in the functions of mind but it is expressed through ways of 'standing, speaking, walking, and thereby of feeling and thinking' (Bourdieu, 1984: 190). Embodiment enables Bourdieu to overcome the binary of structure versus agency in analysing individuals' relationship to the social world for, by his account, the social world is in the body.

The embodiment of identities has been useful in developing class cultural theory through empirical research. Archer and Yamashita (2003: 119) detect agency in boys constructing their identities and evidence this in the forms of speech, style and clothing adopted by the boys. Deliberate cultivation of particular kinds of embodied masculinities would be likely to hinder the social mobility of the boys and the boys themselves recognised that this would be the case, citing their previous experience in job interviews, for example. Their strong attachment, therefore, to a particular locality and their choice to embody and articulate that attachment in their language contributes to the reproduction of inequality and continued oppression.

A dilemma was raised for this study in treating language/dialect as part of the habitus of young participants whose social identities were being considered. They used strong west of Scotland dialects during interviews. The transcriber had been given no guidance as to how these should or should not be represented but, interestingly, had spelled young peoples' speech phonetically to indicate their dialect, while conveying all other participants' speech as standard English. And yet, all participants spoke in dialect of one kind or another. The participant from the Scottish Executive Schools' Division, for example, used a very pronounced East London dialect. It seemed patronising to differentiate young peoples' speech as dialect even though it represented an important and consciously adopted aspect of their identities. To represent all speech as dialect, though, might cause offence to professional and policy staff interviewed. When interviews with young people were translated into standard English, a good deal of the vigour of their speech was lost. Even their meanings seemed to be diminished. Young people's speech is represented further on as the very strong and confident dialect that it is but standard English, rather than phonetic, spellings have been used throughout interview data. In this way it is intended that all particpants' speech is treated respectfully while recognising dialect as an important part – arguably the main semiotic – of local and class identities.

Contention exists as to how far Bourdieuian theory encompasses the possibility of change for individuals and for society. The theory has been criticised for its denial of human agency. Arnot (2002: 49) comments: 'The cultural reproduction of class and sexual identities appears to be a "deep" unconscious process, which, although materially determined, is unlikely to be broken'.

Little prospect is offered of individuals developing a critical awareness of their own habits, attitudes and practices, nor of individuals seeking to break these as part of a broader commitment to change in the social order. For those seeking radical change through, for example, a re-organised school system, there would be little hope against the social determinism of Bourdieu's theory

(Arnot, 2002). Others (Reay, 1995; DiGeorgio, 2009) have argued that there is a dialectical interaction between habitus and field, with each in a process of producing and re-producing their views of the other. Individuals are capable of rational choices when operating in a given context. There is greatest likelihood of rational choices coming into play at times of crisis or disruption.

The schooling of class and gender

What part is played by schools in the formation of pupils' identities? Schools are not just a neutral background or a forum for negotiations about class and gender identities. Studies have shown that schools, too, are actively involved in negotiations of pupil identity. The negotiation of pupil identities within school settings encompasses – for schools – the central construct of ability (Reay and Wiliam, 1999; Hamilton, 2002). Schools impact upon pupil identities through encouraging the internalisation of school and teacher criteria (Broadfoot, 1996) – that is, pupils take to themselves the school's evaluation of them with, for some, a damaging impact on future lives. 'It is the inexplicit, indirect effects of the way schools work that stand out in the long perspective on masculine formation. A stark case is the way streaming and "failure" push groups of working-class boys towards alienation' (Connell, 1989).

The institutional modelling of ability, for example, through the means by which learning and learners are organised (e.g. setting and streaming) places constraints on potential social identities (Ball, 1981; Reay and Wiliam, 1999). Ingram (2009) linked judgements about educational success and failure to boys' attitudes to secondary schooling. In a working-class community in Northen Ireland where the Eleven Plus still applied, boys who failed and were destined for secondary, as opposed to high school, internalised that failure and developed a culture of resistance to school. This experience of rejection consolidated their alignment with their local community. Boys who passed, on the other hand, became ambivalent or resistant to their local community in order to promote their further success (Ingram, 2009: 422). In other UK education systems, comprehensive schools in various forms were seen as a means of addressing problems caused by labelling children as failures at the age of 11 (in England and Wales) and 12 (in Scotland). Comprehensive schools served local communities and reflected those communities. In a context of high social exclusion, their very narrow stratification in some communities has been viewed as operating against the interests of working-class children. Experience here lends further weight to the notion that working-class identities represent a barrier to be overcome if success in education is to be achieved. Ingram notes 'a dialectical confrontation' when a working-class habitus operates in a field different from the one within which it was constructed (Ingram, 2009: 428).

Pupil ability identity is considered to be a dynamic and negotiated construct and, potentially, open to parental influence. Hamilton (2002) researched the extent to which parents' views of their children's abilities affected the negotiation of ability identity in the maintained and the independent school sectors in Scotland. She found that parents of pupils in maintained schools were more likely to look to the school for ability constructs and to have internalised those constructs as they were communicated in grades awarded to their children. 'Parental role in the articulation of ability and interactions with school as well as their perceptions of their own position/role within their education communities seems to have been an integral element in shaping the independence of ability identity' (Hamilton, 2002: 601).

Empirical work on the negotiation of identities in school settings has been successful in showing how schools are actively involved in the processes whereby pupils' identities are negotiated, although schools are not the principal site for such negotiations. Families are party to the negotiations of pupil identity but, as discussed previously in Chapter 2, the form and extent of parental involvement varies considerably according to social class and gender. Hanafin and Lynch (2002), writing about the involvement in education of working-class parents in Ireland, found that, although there was a continuum of parental involvement in schooling, parents at both ends of that continuum were unhappy with the quality of their involvement in spite of their clear desire to participate.

Conclusion

Gender and social class had been found to be invisible in policy in spite of their conspicuousness in exclusion statistics. This chapter set out to examine how sociology theorised gender and social class identities, especially of young people in school settings. Ethnographies, particularly Paul Willis' *Learning to Labour,* addressed a central problem for educational sociologists: why did working-class children fare relatively badly within the education system? Willis showed that the oppositional, anti-school behaviour of the 'lads' in his study related to their development of the protective layers of a culture which would allow them to withstand the impact of life as workers under industrial capitalism. Willis' work was before its time in its demonstration of the development of particular cultural identities, masculine and working class, within economic differentiations. The culture of the 'lads' valorised solidarity with the peer group, placed a high value on humour, and esteemed an ability to resist the controlling demands of arbitrary authority. This behaviour was shown to be deliberately cultivated in relation to the wider social context and to their future lives.

Willis' work questions the extent to which young people were exercising agency in their oppositional behaviour in school settings. Chapters 4, 5 and 6 will relate that question to the experience of excluded pupils. Class cultural identities will be considered in weighing up the relative influences of school and wider social factors in the exclusion of young people.

Within gender analyses, Connell argued that all gender identities were part of a structure of power relations. Masculinities were varied, fluid and continuously negotiated but, more than that, some masculinities were dominant and others subordinate. Heirarchies, or hegemonies, within masculinities were achieved and sustained by processes of 'othering', resulting in alliances and hostilities, inclusion and exclusion. Connell's account of how masculinities are negotiated reflected Willis' account of the 'lads' and the 'ear'oles'. Also like Willis, Connell argued the influence of social class, among other factors, in determining different forms of masculinity. The social class dimension of Connell's theory was not always apparent in some subsequent analyses which drew upon Connell's theory of masculine hegemonies to explain boys' underachievement and challenging behaviour in school settings.

More recent empirical studies have focused on the intersections of class and gender in the processes through which girls and boys negotiated identities in school settings, although there was debate as to whether or not social class was the main formative influence shaping other forms of identity. In a changed world where the traditional, post-school pathways for young working-class men and women were closed, labour markets were no longer important sites for the formation of class identities. These were now very localised, with boys in particular demonstrating very strong attachments to their own communities. Absence of work, and associated travel to the workplace, was seen to have re-inforced strong affiliations to local neighbourhoods. In the absence of traditional industry, boys were using leisure pursuits such as support for the local football team to signal and sustain working-class masculinities. It is intended that the line of enquiry here, informed by understandings of the class cultural identities of girls and boys will yield insights into why working-class boys are disproportionately excluded.

Chapter 4

Excluded pupils and their social identities

'You shouldn't talk like that about Neds. Neds are alright . . .'

In this chapter the broad social identities of excluded pupils are considered using a series of 20 pupil case studies. These were constructed from classroom observation and interviews conducted in four secondary schools and in venues convenient to pupils' families. In addition, a range of documentation was made available by the schools. These data are used here and in two subsequent chapters to address how pupils' negotiation of particular gender and class identities related to their exclusion from school. Those negotiations were shaped by, and compounded, not just differences between pupils but also inequalities within the school system and in Scottish society. Also considered here is how far pupils are exercising agency in the processes leading to their exclusion from school. In other words, to what extent were boys and girls choosing to oppose the processes of schooling? And, if they were, why would they make such a choice? Alternatively, it could be argued that most of the pupils in this study were victims of structural inequalities – that the circumstances in which they lived their lives impelled them towards conflict with the school system. Theories of class cultural identities, especially those using Bourdieu's concept of habitus, have cast new light on the supposed polarity between agency and structure enabling both to be considered simultaneously. In analysing the experience of excluded pupils, a focus will be taken on the interplay between the two.

The discussion will consider the negotiation of social identities in relation to schooling, pupil behaviour and exclusions and will be organised into three chapters and discussed under three main themes emerging from analysis of the data. The analysis of data under themes is arbitrary. The case study data were multifaceted, interconnected and layered. In separating out strands, there was a danger that some of that would be lost. To minimise this, and avoid the deconstruction of case studies, some analysis includes case studies 'in the round' in an effort to convey the wholeness of pupils' experience as it relates to particular themes. Similarly, the division of findings into three chapters is also artificial since some themes cut across the chapter organisers. Chapter 5 deals with exclusions, engagement and participation in schooling; Chapter 6 discusses exclusions and young people's lives. In this chapter the four themes discussed are:

- Multiple and intersecting identities
- Femininities and schooling
- Masculinities and schooling
- Femininities and masculinities.

The economic circumstances of pupils' lives are discussed further on and gender and other identities will be related to social class. The aim in these three findings chapters is to consider the development of class cultural identities and to consider exclusions as part of gendered and 'classed' experience of schooling.

Multiple and intersecting identities

Seventeen of the case study pupils were boys and just three were girls. One pupil, a boy, was reported by his school as 'middle-class' on the basis of his father's occupation and only one pupil, also a boy, was from a black ethnic minority. The case study sample here is a result of school choice and the willingness of pupils to participate but, as it happens, it bears some resemblance to the overall profile of excluded pupils in Scotland. For example, the sample here includes three girls out of twenty pupils when the proportion nationally is one girl for every five pupils excluded. While gender is a main theme of this project, the case study sample gave a clear indication that gender identities were not simple dichotomies. The case study pupils had multiple identities which cut across their gender identities. One such form of identity was drawn from youth culture.

Case study pupils conveyed a strong sense of affiliation to particular subgroups within youth culture, most usually to the Neds. This affiliation is strongly associated with working-class youth and with social exclusion. Originally the term was used by the police to describe those who have criminal associations. It has come to refer to teenagers who gather and socialise in public spaces such as parks and who wear sports-type clothes – hooded sweatshirts, skip caps, track suit trousers tucked into white socks, and trainers. Neds have had a very bad press. Their behaviour has been viewed as threatening to the wider community, deserving of Anti-Social Behaviour Orders and justifying the use of curfews for young people under 16. In spite of this, case study pupils asserted their Ned identity as a matter of pride. Most of the case study pupils referred to themselves as 'Neds' and consciously asserted that identity. Kat, for example, at the start of the school session, had 'point-blank' refused to work with a group of girls who were Moshers (Goth-type style, black nail varnish, etc.) because of their style. Kat claimed that she liked to beat them up at weekends and so could not work in a group with them. One boy was offended when Neds were referred to disparagingly by the drama teacher: 'You shouldn't talk like that about Neds. Neds are alright.'

Dress or the general style of girls and boys allowed their Ned identities to be clearly manifested, often creating a source of conflict with teachers. Ned identities entailed the adoption of deliberately oppositional attitudes to teachers and to school. For example, one case study pupil was repeatedly told to remove his skip cap in lessons until, eventually, the cap was confiscated. Usually, 'Ned' pupils managed to reach an accommodation whereby certain items of clothing would be accepted, even though all four schools required school uniform. Not only was dress used to convey class affiliations but dress enabled young people to convey gender oppositions within a common alignment and could be varied according to the social setting: 'she wears make-up when she goes out and she doesn't wear make-up when she's playing football and stuff like that, when she's fighting' (Eddie).

For boys as well, there were differences in presentation depending on the social occasion:

> like most boys only wear jeans when they are going out, like going into the dancing or something and if they are, they spike their hair up, or at least comb it or brush it, wear a hat or something like that, and put aftershave and that on . . . Well, you look at boys and see if they are wearing shirt and jeans with boots and all their jewellery, then that means they're going out and see how if you see them in trackies with their hats up to here, then they are not going anywhere, they are just sloping about their own scheme looking for trouble.
>
> (Eddie)

Dress and physical presentation were used as markers of identity. In the case of Neds, this identity was rooted in social class culture, arguably distinguishing Ned identity from other kinds of youth 'style'. There was a sense in which the re-appropriation of the term 'Ned' was a conscious attempt to assert a particular working-class identity associated with social exclusion. Given the tendency to blame particular groups for the disadvantage they experience, the response of young people here could be seen as admirably confident.

Strong attachments to their own neighbourhoods formed an important aspect of young people's identities. Case study pupils articulated a sense of belonging to a particular locality as constituting an important part of their identities – references to 'my bit' were frequent. This linked to their need to feel safe, to be known and accepted (Nayak, 2003), but there was evidence that a sense of belonging to one place was accompanied by a strong sense of not belonging to other places. Territorial conflicts figured largely in the lives of girls and boys interviewed and were at times the cause of their exclusion. One assistant headteacher (AHT) from a secondary school spoke of an increase in gang warfare as a result of a tragic accident when an 11-year-old boy had been killed on the M8 motorway while being chased during territorial fighting. Reprisals had been ongoing and had involved a number of boys at the school, resulting in their exclusion.

Local or territorial affiliations cut across gender and other oppositions. Girls saw themselves as having a strong connection to place and this connection served to align them with boys from the same neighbourhood. In the case of local gang fights, the main divisions were portrayed as territorial and involved girls and boys. Mostly boys were involved in these gang fights but not exclusively. Eddie gave an example: 'sometimes there are lassies from other schemes and like, the lassies from my bit, sometimes they will go and fight with them but they are based on – like a team?'

Eddie, one of the case study boys, indicated the complexities of oppositions and allegiances affecting girls and boys. He explained that some of his girl friends were 'real lassies, like pure all glammed up and that', but most of them were tomboys. When asked which would be most likely to experience trouble in school or elsewhere, Eddie replied, 'Tomboys because they have got more brain like a boy than a lassie. And it's like . . . see boys and girls that come from a scheme that fight with another scheme, they always end up getting involved'.

The term favoured by the press is 'ladette' rather than the longer-established 'tomboy'. Jackson (2006a) characterised the main distinction between the two as the overtly (hetero)sexualised image of 'ladettes'. Whatever the term, there was evidence that some of the femininities admired by case study pupils were active, aggressive and highly visible in public spaces.

Nayak (2003) described how football was a means through which identity was negotiated by young men in the north-east of England. Similarly, girls and boys in this study conveyed their support for particular football clubs by wearing football tops so that they were visible under school-approved sweatshirts. In Scotland, affiliations, especially but not exclusively to Glasgow Celtic and Glasgow Rangers Football Clubs, have been associated with 'religious hatred and sectarian bigotry' (Scottish Executive, 2002). Sectarianism has been perceived as a problem in Scotland for generations (Devine, 2000) with the Executive introducing legislation in 2003 that specifically targeted sectarian behaviour in Section 74 of the Criminal Justice (Scotland) Act. For some case study pupils, wearing football tops signalled not just support for a particular club but also a Catholic or a Protestant identity. These affiliations transcended gender dichotomies and sometimes drew boys and girls into violence. Eddie told of the Orange Walk coming through H—, the predominantly Catholic area where he lived. Eddie spoke admiringly of Kelly:

> It was when the Orange Walk was walking through H— and Kelly was wearing a Celtic top and other girls [following the Walk] were wearing Rangers' tops . . . She held up her badge [on the football top] and kissed it and all the lassies walked over to her ready to fight her. She – Kelly – she

> battered six of them herself . . . She is like a tomboy but sometimes she can be like a girl.
>
> (Eddie)

Territorial and sectarian motives were hard to separate out here. H— was traditionally a Catholic and a poorer area. The routing of the Orange Walk through such a community was intended as, and would be viewed as, provocative. Eddie attends a Catholic secondary school, and for some members of his local community, especially the younger ones, Kelly's actions would be seen as heroic.

For young people in the West of Scotland, football colours may be intended to convey a Protestant or Catholic identity and there were some signs that these aspects of identity were consolidated by the existence of denominational (Catholic) and non-denominational (Protestant) schools within the state system in Scotland. For example, exclusions had resulted from boys (including several case study pupils) from the Catholic secondary going at lunchtime to a nearby non-denominational school to seek a fight. This is not to argue here that the existence of that system causes sectarian conflict, but that young people seeking to define themselves and others used that affiliation as a strong signifier of commonality or difference.

Nationally, Scottish Executive statistics (Scottish Government, 2009a) show that pupils from minority ethnic groups generally had lower exclusion rates than white-UK pupils, although rates varied widely across different ethnic groups. Just one of the case study pupils was from a black ethnic minority group. The scope of this study does not encompass ethnic identities and school exclusions. However, racism emerged as contentious issue in the experience of one pupil, Raj, who was in S3. During the interview, he was pleasant but very shy and unforthcoming. He was noted as keeping a low profile in class and around the school and as being fairly passive during lessons. Raj came to Hammond High School on a placing request because his older brother was already in the school, working hard and doing well. However, the deputy headteacher (DHT) described Raj as 'a strange, strange boy' who had done some 'stupid' things that had got him into trouble. Raj had some friends but they were described as 'falling out' on a regular basis. Raj had made allegations of racist abuse against these friends but the school felt that this was part of the teasing that went on in this friendship group and that Raj had reciprocated with other insults. The DHT said that most of the dealings he had with Raj were through racist things:

> Raj said somebody (Stuart) called him 'a black shit' and that James had punched him during maths . . . Stuart did not deny it . . . he said that Raj had been annoying him and had called him fat. Raj is very much into name-calling. He will claim someone has made a racist remark . . . about him but when you investigate it, you find he has given as good as he gets.
>
> (DHT)

The DHT was quite clear that Raj was not a victim of intentional racism. This claim sits uncomfortably with research into the experiences of black and minority ethnic pupils following the transition to secondary school (Caulfield and Hill, 2002). In that study, also conducted in the West of Scotland, pupils reported that peer racism increased between primary and secondary school and that, although teachers were seen to have a key role in dealing with racist incidents, they were often ineffective in doing so. Raj himself says that he was happy in secondary school, preferring it to primary because he liked to have different teachers and to be able to leave the school premises at lunchtime. He liked the extra freedom available at secondary school. In addition, he was at this school as a result of a placing request. His parents had chosen the school because Raj's older brother was happy there.

Action against racism here is problematic. Raj was clearly experiencing racist abuse but neither he nor his family objected in any public way. Neither did the school feel that there was anything untoward happening. Scotland's school population was overwhelmingly white at 96.35 per cent in 2004, according to official statistics (Scottish Executive, 2005). Black ethnic minority families are concentrated in particular inner city areas and so some schools would have a much higher proportion of black pupils. None of the four case study schools was in that position. Raj's family were very conspicuous in the area where they lived and in the schools they used. It is possible that they desired to be assimilated into the community and so tolerated unreasonable circumstances rather than make a fuss or draw attention to themselves. This interpretation is supported by Raj's mother's reaction to his exclusion. He had been excluded just once for a short period of time but it had caused Raj and his family great embarrassment. Raj's mother declined to participate in an interview but she gave permission for Raj to be interviewed.

The complexity of the identities pursued by young people in this study points to how important out-of-school influences were for adolescents. The simple gender dichotomies evident in strategies to tackle boys' relatively low attainment have attributed this to 'laddishness' and have neglected the alignments and 'otherings' pursued by girls and boys. Some of these, such as sectarian identities, are long-standing in Scotland but others are the result of the impact of social and cultural change. This point will be developed further on, after the feminine and masculine identities of the case study pupils have been more fully examined.

Femininities and schooling

Girls account for just 20 per cent of school exclusions and just 3 of the 20 case studies were girls. The relatively low rate of girls' exclusion raises questions about exclusions and femininities:

- What are the reasons for girls' exclusions?

- How does the negotiation of femininities relate to exclusions?
- Are girls who are excluded acting out femininities differently from other girls?

Further on in this chapter, girls' exclusions will be compared with boys' exclusions. These questions will be considered here through the case studies of three girls, Gill, Kat and Lorraine, who came from three different secondary schools. In addition to having been excluded, the girls had a number of factors in common: they were approximately of the same age, they were working class and they were recognised by their teachers as having abilities in a number of subjects.

The girls: Gill, Lorraine and Kat

Gill was 15 years old and very articulate during the interview. She lived with her mother, an older sister, a younger sister who was in S1 at the same school and two younger brothers who were still in nursery. Gill's business studies teacher knew her very well and spoke of how much she liked her. The teacher described herself as having a soft spot for Gill. When this teacher was asked why Gill had been in trouble for her behaviour, she was mystified. She did say, however, that Gill had a group of friends – girls – who, among staff, were seen as quite challenging to teachers. This teacher's view of Gill was one of several examples of some excluded pupils being seen quite differently, and much more positively, by certain teachers who clearly had a good relationship with pupils in difficulty elsewhere. This applied to pupils who were excluded on multiple occasions as well as to pupils who had been in less trouble. An important aspect of schooling is its capacity to provide pupils with opportunities for positive and constructive relationships with adults. For some pupils in particular, that opportunity may be the difference between their engagement with education and complete disaffection. This point will be developed further on in relation to a case study boy who had been excluded on numerous occasions and implications will be drawn then.

Lorraine was aged 14 and lived with her mother and her stepfather. Relationships at home had been difficult for a year or so with Lorraine's mother at times threatening to put her out of the house. Lorraine's relationship with her stepfather had been particularly difficult, causing Lorraine's mother to contact the Social Work Department to seek help in managing Lorraine and her very wilful behaviour. Lorraine had been excluded for the first time in April of S3. The exclusion had been for just two days and had resulted from Lorraine swearing at a teacher. Although she had only ever been excluded once, Lorraine had been in trouble at other times for loud, boisterous and sometimes aggressive behaviour. Her teachers linked this behaviour to her appearance:

> Well, she's a big bruiser, for want of a better word. I mean she comes up the stairs and you can hear her bouncing along corridors and such and she's banging off both the walls, you know, bang, bang, bang.
>
> (Business studies teacher)

Her guidance teacher offered a similar view of Lorraine's image 'She's a big girl. She's loud. She can be aggressive. That has surfaced probably more this year than it ever has done in the past' (Guidance teacher).

Across the range of interviews with teachers about girls and boys, this was the only instance where a young person's body was treated as an appropriate matter for comment and, more than that, as the source of problematic behaviour. The guidance teacher went on to suggest that Lorraine's physical appearance had caused her to adopt a 'tough' identity:

> My opinion is that she wants to be an individual, as a lot of pupils of that age do. Her size and her stature, I think, could make it quite difficult for her to fit in with the way that a lot of girls look. And she is making an attempt, I think, to make a statement about 'I am an individual. I am a female and here is how I want to look' and she's not afraid of authority as such. She wants to fit in but she is obviously not afraid of getting into trouble. She has been able to stand up to her mother and say, 'I am wearing this'.
>
> (Guidance teacher)

Lorraine differed from the other girls and from many of the other case study samples in that her attendance was very good. It stood at 95 per cent for the session in which the research was conducted and Lorraine indicated that she was very happy in school.

Kat had had numerous exclusions. She had just started S3 at the time of the research. She lived with her mother and her older sister who was 17 and at college. The family received support from the Social Work Department, mostly in relation to welfare rights and benefits but also to make sure that 'mum was okay and that the family situation was settled' (family support worker). Kat's mother was on a methadone programme at the time of the research. Her partner had been very ill during the previous year and there were indications that a very stressful home life had impacted on Kat's experience of school. The family support worker had worked with Kat in a group work situation after school for a 10-week period and knew her well. She indicated that Kat's well-being was very much tied up with her mother's well-being and vice-versa. Kat had never been excluded in primary school but had been excluded a number of times in S1 and S2. The DHT said that the school had taken Kat under its wing early in S1. She had been one of six pupils to be given support in a behaviour support group run in the school by specialist teachers from the local behaviour support base. All of the other members of the group were boys. In S3 Kat still attended the base for part of her timetable. Her behaviour was reported as having improved but there were still episodes where she gave backchat to teachers during lessons, leading to an escalating confrontation and her eventual exclusion.

Two of the case study girls had poor attendance but this did not seem to reflect a broader 'withdrawal' from school processes for, when present, all three were highly visible in lessons. This is reflected in the reasons why they had got into difficulty – all three girls were noted as shouting, swearing and giving cheek to teachers. For example, loud and aggressive behaviour was reported by Gill's history teacher who recounted how Gill had been caught cheating in a test. Gill, when accused of this, had 'nearly thrown a fit', shouting that she was not cheating. She had been excluded just once in S3 for 2.5 days. With her friend, she had stolen some blackboard cleaning materials because it was Guy Fawkes' night and the material was easily flammable. Her friend had put the materials in Gill's bag. Gill was caught with them and excluded, although her friend was not. In Gill's view, her exclusion had been fair but she felt that her friend should also have been excluded. Gill reported that she had almost been excluded again around that time when her teacher had not allowed her to go to the toilet, although she had a particular reason to go. Gill had responded by shouting at this teacher and had been reported for her behaviour. 'Getting on' or not with teachers emerged as a big part of the girls' experience of school. The accounts by teachers showed that all three girls were viewed very differently by different teachers.

Of the three girls Kat had been excluded most often by far. The DHT reported that her exclusions were caused by talking back to teachers – 'She just wouldn't take a telling'. Kat herself said these exclusions were for 'just being cheeky and all that and answering back'. All of her exclusions were for classroom misbehaviour. She was reported as being in less trouble but, the day before she was interviewed, she had told the History teacher to shut up. Kat did not seem to seek confrontation with teachers but she also seemed unable to allow them to tell her what to do. 'She just really finds it difficult to step back – and then she is excluded' (Family support worker). The most frequent reason for exclusion in Scotland was general and persistent disobedience. Kat's exclusions all fell into that category.

The incident where Lorraine was excluded came about after a referral for not wearing school uniform. Lorraine was already angry about having been sent to the AHT in this instance because she felt there were other pupils also not wearing uniform. Perceptions of the fairness of sanctions, including exclusions, emerged as a key issue for pupils. In Lorraine's case, the situation escalated when the AHT phoned Lorraine's mother to say she was being sent home to change.

> . . . I was pulled up for something . . . I think it was my uniform . . . I swore at him so he phoned my mum and said I was to go home.
>
> (Lorraine)

This behaviour was judged to merit an exclusion – the only one Lorraine had ever had. Her exclusion seemed to have arisen from her anguish that further pressure would be put upon her mother as a result of Lorraine's transgression.

The girls were very clear about which teachers they liked and did not like and this was related to how far they felt they were treated respectfully by their teachers. However, there was an issue here in that there were different understandings of what constituted respectful behaviour. Some of Gill's teachers, for example, indicated that respectful behaviour, according to Gill, was often too familiar for their liking:

> Gill does not like to be told anything at all. She very much speaks to you in the way she speaks to her friends, I think. That has become an issue . . .
> (History teacher)

The same judgement applied to Kat. She, too, was judged to respond inappropriately to teachers and yet neither girl had been excluded in primary school. Their behaviour may have changed with adolescence or the tone of teacher/pupil interchanges in secondary may have been different. The girls' demands that they be treated respectfully by teachers had much in common with boys who were trying to negotiate masculinities which were powerful and high-status among their peer group. 'Respect' is considered further in relation to case study boys.

How does the negotiation of femininities relate to exclusions? There were indications that girls exercised choice in how they represented their femininity. Sometimes they dressed to distinguish themselves from boys, while at other times they emphasised their alignment based on, for example, girls' and boys' sense of belonging to the same locality. Eddie, one of the case study boys, explained the variations in how girls presented themselves: 'See when she's fighting, she's a tomboy, or see when she wants to play football, she's a tomboy, but see when she's going to the dancing or going out with her pals, she's a lassie'.

The distinction drawn here by Eddie conveys a sense from the data that girls acted out multiple femininities and that some ways of doing femininity, ways that led to exclusion, encompassed assertiveness and aggression. None of the case study girls had been excluded for fighting or violence but there was indirect evidence of girls behaving in these ways. Some of the exclusions imposed on case study boys had been because of fighting others from a different area. Girls, too, saw themselves as having a strong connection to place and this connection served to align them with boys from the same neighbourhood.

The alignment of girls and boys with each other and in opposition to others could also be seen in classroom contexts where girls and boys would be part of the same social group and where that group was the challenging one for the teacher. One home economics lesson observed provided such an example. In that lesson, Kat seemed motivated and happy. There were only ten pupils in this class, two of whom were boys, and there were two groups. Most girls stood quietly at the back of the class, watching the other group, which contained Kat and the boys, carrying on. Kat moved about a lot. She was very gregarious – *That's the most revolting thing I have ever tasted in my life* – but seemed to be purposeful in getting the task done. She asked me if I would like to taste her spaghetti carbonara but I declined. One of the boys, her friend, asked if this was a judgement of her cooking. They were very playful and not at all confrontational but they dominated the space. The lesson observed demonstrated some boys and all girls, except for Kat, occupying the peripheries of the classroom. Kat's behaviour with regard to classroom space was exactly like the behaviour of the boys.

Some femininities had much in common with boys but within these common allegiances, there was evidence of boys 'othering' of girls. While Eddie described common aspects of identity between boys and girls, he differentiated between the female and the male members of his 'team' in their competence at fighting. 'We throw bricks and bottles and sticks and all that but lassies, they just walk into it and pull hair and all that.'

Thus, even where particular and aggressive feminine behaviours were admired by boys (so long as they were part of the same 'team'), they were simultaneously disparaged. This echoes the point made by commentators (Reay, 2001; Francis, 2005) that, although there are multiple femininities, what they all have in common is their deferment of power to the boys. Alongside that, some girls used their friendships with boys to support the negotiation of particular kinds of femininity – more assertive, loud and dominant than other girls in classrooms and other spaces. They might have been termed 'ladettes' – their behaviour corresponded to popular notions of 'ladette' behaviour – but this word was never used in the course of the study. These girls were 'masculine' but there was some indication that friendships with boys provided scope for girls to be girls in ways challenging to normative femininities. The evidence here is too limited to develop this interpretation.

Are girls who are excluded acting out femininities differently from other girls? There has been a tendency in the literature to dichotomise girls' and boys' problem behaviour. Boys' behaviour is represented generally as 'acting out' – being loud and disruptive of other activity. Girls, on the other hand, have been generally represented as 'acting in', their difficulties manifesting themselves as eating disorders or depression, for example. The behaviour of the case study girls ran counter to this description. Their behaviour differed from general accounts of girls' 'problem' behaviour. The case study girls differed, too, from the behaviour of other girls whose behaviour was not regarded as problematic but who were noted (Osler *et al.* 2002) as using tearfulness and remorse as ways of deflecting possible sanctions. When challenged about some aspect of their behaviour or thwarted in some way in their wishes, the case study girls were far from remorseful, instead they shouted and swore in response to teacher decisions. In their avoidance of 'stereotypical' feminine behaviour, the case study girls increased the likelihood of their being excluded.

The case study girls differed, too, from some descriptions of 'problem' girl behaviour as characterised by withdrawal from school processes (Ridge, 2005; Osler *et al.* 2002). While in school, the girls in this study were reported as having friends and being popular. Classroom observation similarly showed the girls to be socially well-integrated. Two of the case study girls had poor attendance but this did not intimate a broader pattern of withdrawal from school but linked to the demands placed upon them by family circumstances. Their participation in schooling, especially Kat's, in personal circumstances not supportive of education, could be seen as indicative of strong engagement and even as a triumph of individual agency.

The experience of the case study girls showed that they experienced neither a loss of voice nor of agency in their engagement with schooling. Their exclusions in all cases came about because of their preparedness to challenge verbally and publicly the authority of teachers. Adolescent girls generally may experience a lessening of their powers of agency but the data here points to differences between girls and, especially, to the reason why so few girls are excluded and why some are. A key difference between the case study girls and others was that excluded girls were prepared to challenge authority. Many of the case study sample and their families were socially marginalised. Against that background, girls' challenging behaviour could be seen as feistiness, as resistance to unreasonable circumstances. Girls shared that wider social exclusion with most of the boys, providing a sound basis for cross-gender alignments. Jackson (2006b: 23) has raised the possibility that girls as well as boys might be stigmatised by their peer group for pursuing learning and academic achievement in school. Friendships with boys may have facilitated the 'doing' of femininities in particular ways, especially in Kat's case, with behaviours leading to exclusion and alienation from academic achievement. But those negotiations and affiliations also need to be contextualised in the wider social marginalisation of case study pupils.

Masculinities and schooling

The 17 boys in this study were distinguished one from another by a number of factors, but the question to be considered here is how far their formal exclusion from school occurred as part of a process by which they were negotiating their gender and class identities. This section will first discuss hegemonic masculinities, the means by which they were negotiated and the relationship between those negotiations and exclusion from school. The second part of this section will consider 'other' masculinities and the links there to school exclusions.

Gramsci's theory of political hegemonies has provided a means of understanding the dynamic by which some boys claim and sustain a leading position in social life (Connell, 1995: 77). For decades, the concept of dominant masculinities has been particularly useful in analysing the negotiation of gendered identities in school settings. For example, Willis (1978) showed how the boys in his study were actively constructing social class relations during the last two years of schooling and doing so in relation to their gender and social class identities. Arnot (2003: 103), reviewing the impact of Willis' study, noted that Willis had shown the ways in which different masculinities, and particular forms of hegemonic masculinity were created, regulated and reproduced within the same school. The concept is used here to understand better the over-representation of boys in exclusion statistics. Working-class boys, disadvantaged socially and economically, sought to negotiate for themselves identities that accorded power and status with the peer group and from their own communities. The discussion will be pursued here with reference to two case study boys in particular, Andy and Ross, both of whom were engaged in negotiating dominant masculinities.

Andy

A number of the boys in this study exercised considerable control over their personal lives, sometimes well beyond what would be accorded to other adolescents, and in marked contrast to the scope for control offered by their schools. For example, 12-year-old Andy and his brother, Craig, were living with their mother who had mental health problems and who had great difficulty in helping her sons to organise their lives. The boys came to secondary school with what the DHT called 'an absolutely horrific report' from their primary school indicating a range of concerns, including some raised by the local police: 'Caught with drugs. Kept in cell overnight because no responsible adult could be found to take them. They have den where they sleep overnight' (extract from police report to Andy's primary school).

The boys seemed to have exercised a great deal of control over their own lives. For example, Andy and his brother refused a referral to the educational psychologist, even though their mother and the school were advocating this course. The boys were hostile to professionals. They preferred not to have a social worker and were strongly opposed to other professionals entering their lives. There was, though, great concern, about the experience of the boys out of school. They were known to a range of community services, including police and social workers – 'They are so well known to everyone these boys, to the police, to everyone' (DHT). Andy's mother had reported to the school that, at home, he had been violent towards her, swearing at her and kicking her. The boys were reported to have put their mother out of the house on occasion. Andy himself has no real explanation to offer when asked why he gets into bother – 'I don't know. I haven't a clue'. He knows that he himself sometimes tries to annoy the teacher but he also feels that sometimes it is the teacher's fault. Andy was represented as bright and very engaged by some teachers but there was evidence that he used some lessons to further negotiate a very dominant and controlling masculinity. Andy's French teacher, a young woman, commented on his behaviour in S1:

> Last year, it was horrendous. Andy led the class as it were. He would tell people, you know, it was him, he was the King. And you know, he strutted in my class . . . That is how he would do it. He would strut into class and his behaviour was awful.
>
> (French teacher)

This teacher also said that Andy was very bright, had a lovely French accent and with one-to-one coaching could be really good at French.

Andy was formally recorded as excluded just once in S1, but during an interview he said he had been excluded six times, all in S1. Later, the DHT explained that the single exclusion given to Andy was in line with the local authority policy of not excluding pupils wherever possible. He also explained that Andy had been 'sent home' a number of times pending his mother coming to the school to discuss his behaviour. She would usually come on the following day. 'Sending home' would not count as a formal exclusion and so this practice would account for the disparity between Andy's account and the school's account on the one hand and the written record on the other hand.

Ross

The second case study is Ross who was 13 and who lived with his mother and his older brother. Ross's attendance in S1 had been poor. His record showed 129 absences from a possible 369 openings (half-days) at time of interview, giving an attendance rate of 65.04 per cent. Ross had been excluded just once, for one day, during S1. This was surprising given accounts of his behaviour in school but his poor attendance, and the 'sending home' mechanism, might explain this to some extent. His father had access to the family home and Ross had a good deal of contact with him. Ross's father had wider family in the area and they were reported as being well known locally. Ross's relationship to his father and his father's family were reported to have made Ross himself very streetwise. Ross was tall and looked mature for a 13-year-old. His friends were older but it was reported by several staff that he did not seem out of place, physically or socially, in the company of 16- and 17-year-old boys. This marked him out in a group of first-year boys: 'he has got to be the big guy and you can see the fear factor with some of the other kids' (Home/school link worker).

Ross did not appear to have friends in his own class in school. His male classmates seemed to regard him with a mixture of admiration and deference. One teacher indicated that Ross was very protective of people in the class, offering to 'get' anyone who bullied his fellow classmates.

'Respect' and control

The behaviour which led to the exclusion of both boys could be interpreted as part of the negotiation of hegemonic masculinities. There was evidence from the case studies of how such identities were negotiated through interactions with teachers and with peers in the school setting. Most of the pupils in this study had been excluded, and sometimes repeatedly so, for their very challenging attitudes towards teachers. Teachers cited the disrespect and abuse they experienced from pupils as a main justification for exclusions. In 2007/08, the verbal abuse of staff was the second most common reason for exclusion from school (Scottish Government, 2009a). On the other hand, pupils in this study cited teachers' attitudes to them as the reason why they 'lost it', resulting in their exclusion. Again and again, boys and girls in this study accounted for some of their exclusions by saying that they were responding to being shouted at or being treated with disrespect by their teachers. For example 'The teachers do not treat you right. In Primary 7 the teachers treated you with respect. Here they don't; they treat you like you were dirt, nearly every single teacher' (S1 pupil).

An S3 pupil who had been frequently excluded explained why he sometimes lost all control. 'I can't stand teachers in my face shouting at me. . . . At C— Primary. The teachers were always shouting at me so I always shouted back, swearing and all different things. So I always got suspended' (S3 pupil).

In general, pupils' angry reactions to being shouted at were seen as indicative of a loss of control but there were also indications that some boys were able to use their angry reactions to reach an accommodation with teachers. One teacher, a young woman, commented on how she had learned to deal with Andy, the first case study pupil:

> My experience of Andy was very simple. If you were too antagonistic with him he would react in a similarly antagonistic way and that happened once – the first time I met him. . . . He was showing off to other people and we hit a brick wall quite quickly. He reacted and he was quite aggressive. His body language was quite aggressive. I quickly learned from that if you are full on, he will just shout back at you. He will actually use expressions like 'Don't speak to me like that' or 'Don't shout at me'.
>
> (English teacher)

The teacher went on to say that she now treated Andy differently from other pupils in the class, in that she would not now speak sharply to him. She recognised that there were inequities here but she felt that other pupils in the class expected Andy to be treated differently and therefore did not object. This teacher's changed behaviour could be seen as an example of how teachers, as well as pupils, learn in classrooms. They develop their professional practice to accommodate the diverse range of pupils in each class. However, it is also possible to interpret this teacher's experience as learned deference to a boy who is consciously seeking to be dominant in the classroom, even when the teacher is present.

Similarly, a young woman teacher of another case study boy described a similar experience. The pupil, who had been excluded frequently, indicated that one of the few teachers he got on with was this home economics teacher. The pupil was a boxer and he had invited her to his next boxing match and she was uncertain about whether or not she should go. She had discussed the question with her boyfriend the previous evening and she felt that, if she did not go, Charlie would be offended. There was a risk here of the teacher endorsing Charlie's very particular kind of masculine identity. More than that, as an attractive young woman, the teacher could become a kind of 'scalp' for Charlie. It seemed that Charlie had not invited any other teachers in this way. There seemed to be an issue with authority and respect. Charlie's home economics teacher reported that he wanted to speak to her on equal terms as a friend and he was very offended when she told him that she was not his friend. She could have a positive relationship with him but only if she abandoned the authority lent to her by her position as a teacher.

Power and status

Ross, the second case study pupil, used classroom events and interactions as a means of constructing in a continuing way his identity. This was observed during a history lesson when Ross demonstrated his ability to orchestrate the lesson. Ross sat at the front of the class, in clear view of everyone and close to the teacher. From my seat at the back of the classroom it was clear that Ross used his position to establish himself as the leader of disruptive behaviour. It was apparent that others in the class looked to Ross for their lead. Ross was literally laid back during the lesson, leaning back with his feet on a chair and his hands clasped behind his head. He asked a girl at the other side of the room for a drink from her bottle of Irn-Bru. This was thrown from one pupil to another until it reached Ross. He drank and then threw it back across the room. The teacher did not challenge Ross in a direct way. Instead, he went twice to have a quiet word with him. This tactic had no effect. Ross continued to run the lesson for his own and others' enjoyment, making noises and asking superfluous questions. In fact, the teacher seemed to try to establish an accommodation with Ross. For example, he had refused permission for one of Ross's classmates to go to the toilet. When Ross asked he was granted permission immediately.

Ross did not appear to have friends in his class in school. One of his teachers commented: 'Pupils want to be his friend because I think it is the power he has outwith the school, or the perceived power he has outwith school' (Teacher).

The teacher indicated that Ross was very protective of people in the class and was powerful enough to be able to offer patronage to other boys. This was not heroic altruism, although Ross constructed it as such, but was a means for Ross to demonstrate and to advance further his control and his status.

For a number of the boys, the negotiation of their masculinities involved the establishment of relationships with pupils and teachers where the boys were accepted as dominant. There was evidence that most boys within the case study sample coveted high-status masculinities and that some of their difficulties, and some of their exclusions, arose in the pursuit of those masculinities. For example, the mother of one of the case study pupils, Sam, attributed the change in his behaviour between primary and secondary school to his need to gain the respect of his peer group:

> I think he was just trying to be one of the boys – 'I can do as well as you can do'. If they got into a fight, he would get into a fight, stupid things that really led to him clowning about. Most of it is just stupid with him.
> (Sam's mother)

There was also some indication that Sam was trying to protect himself by gaining a reputation for being 'hard' and that bad behaviour in school enabled him to do that:

> a lot of the kids around here are quite aggressive and all the rest of it. I do not think Sam copes with that very well, like confrontation . . . He would rather talk his way out of a fight than actually get into one.
> (Sam's mother)

The negotiation of these masculinities brought power and status within the peer group to the boys concerned. Although exclusion brought difficulties, especially for case study pupils' families, 'bad boy' masculinities helped to cement friendships and brought enjoyment of life for those who espoused them (Archer and Yamashita, 2003).

'Other' masculinities

Some boys among the case study sample did not enjoy the advantages of 'bad boy' masculinities, even though the rate of their exclusion was very high indeed. The experience of two boys, Ewen and Dougie, will be considered here. Both were largely shunned by their peer group, although Ewen, in particular, seemed to be trying and failing to negotiate more powerful and high-status masculinity.

Ewen

Unusually for pupils in this sample, and for excluded pupils generally, Ewen came from a middle-class and affluent family. The AHT indicated that Ewen's mother and father were both in professional jobs. He had two older brothers aged 22 and 24, one of whom had done well at university and the other who had also graduated with a good degree and started a career. Ewen's exclusions were frequent and increasingly lengthy. During the 2002/03 session, he had been excluded for 31 days in total and was reported by the DHT to be approaching permanent exclusion from St Thomas's High School. Exclusions had been useless in changing Ewen's behaviour but they had provided respite for the school.

Ewen was tall and well built. His physique would indicate that he would play sports but he seemed not to have that interest in common with many boys in the school. Ewen reported that he had never really been happy in school, not even in primary school:

> I just felt as if I had never had any friends or anything like that. Like every single time we played football I got told to go away. The janny [janitor/caretaker] did not particularly like me and my mum went up to the school to complain because he always used to . . . like, when I was younger he always used to slag me when I was at school and my mum went up to complain to the headteacher because he used to talk about me in front of everyone.
> (Ewen)

Ewen's difficulties had continued in secondary school. The DHT reported that, in S1, he had been moved from one class to another because his family contended that it was other pupils in the classes who were leading Ewen into trouble. Ewen cited a number of occasions when he had been bullied or harassed and said this was especially likely to happen on the playing fields and when playing football. The educational psychologist had been involved in working with Ewen's family in the family support group. The referral here had come about because of Ewen's inappropriate tactile behaviour, especially in physical education. At the time of the research Ewen had been referred to the Department of Children's and Family Psychiatry at a nearby hospital.

Ewen's difficulties in his relationships with other boys started, according to Ewen, in Primary 5. This seems to have been the time when his sense of difference, of alienation from other boys was first felt. It did seem that many of the difficulties he had experienced since then were an attempt to gain acceptance from his peer group. For example, Ewen was described as craving attention and of doing quite outlandish things in lessons to get attention. Ewen's drama teacher in S1 and S2 reported that he had brought with him a long history of antagonism from other pupils:

> They hated, they absolutely hated his attention-seeking. To them he would wreck all their work. He would step in and wreck it. He would constantly bicker and moan and in a crybaby fashion that his point of view was not being heard.
> (Drama teacher)

Ewen's teachers made the point that Ewen is very much in control of himself – the behaviour which gets him excluded is not the result of anger or 'losing it' at any time. He seemed to be making a conscious decision to behave or to misbehave.

Dougie

Along with Ewen, Dougie had one of the highest rates of exclusion among the case study sample. Unlike Ewen, he seemed not to be aiming for high-status masculinity within his peer group. The DHT indicated that Dougie was very interested in dancing and had considerable talent. He was a dance teacher in his aunt's disco dancing class and was interested in a career in dance and/or drama. Dougie's father was reported as strongly disapproving of his son's dancing and there was considerable friction between father and son about this. Within school, too, there were indications that Dougie was put under pressure from other boys because of his interests and his style. During a residential stay, the home/school link worker reported that Dougie was the butt of criticism:

> He is effeminate and all that. Dougie can be quite feminine in his speech and in his actions. You can imagine the flack he was getting from G [a fellow male pupil, described as very vocal] and they were sharing a room. But they worked it out and everything was fine.
> (Home/school link worker)

In S3, Dougie had been excluded nine times, one time for 15 days and other times for periods of 11 days. Altogether in S3, he had missed 57 days of school through exclusion, that is 114 openings or half-days out of a possible 390 openings. He was reported as very disruptive in classrooms, refusing to work and adopting a hectoring and aggressive attitude to some of his teachers. He could become very angry and interrupted teachers. Sometimes, he would not stay in his seat. His behaviour seemed to be worse in some subjects – the French Department had referred Dougie a number of times. The home/school link worker believed that Dougie's acting out and aggressive behaviour was part of an attempt to bottle up his feelings:

> there is certainly an attention side to it . . . and act that out and I think that maybe has been his problem. I think he has got to show aggression to make up for the fact that he is different from everybody else. Whether that is the deep root of it, I do not know.
> (Home/school link worker)

The DHT reported that a further exclusion could see Dougie being removed from the school altogether and asked to enrol elsewhere.

Both Ewen and Dougie were socially isolated in school. For them, challenging behaviour and exclusion did not assist in the creation of 'bad boy' status within their peer group. Their identities were troubling to them, to their peers and to their teachers and there were no means through which these issues could be discussed other than through the formal pastoral and discipline referral systems of their school.

Gender differences in exclusions

The main difference between boys' and girls' exclusion was in the extent to which they were excluded. Case study girls' experience of exclusion differed from boys in the study in that they were excluded less often and for shorter periods of time. There were just three girls in this study and two of them had been excluded just once. In all cases, the reasons for their exclusion seemed very similar to the reasons why boys were excluded. In Scotland in 2003/04, the main reason for all exclusions was 'general or persistent disobedience' and 25 per cent of all exclusions were for that reason. The second largest group of exclusions was for verbal abuse of staff and 22 per cent of exclusions were in this category. The girls' exclusions came under these main categories. In that respect, the reason for their exclusions was the same as for a large number of boys' exclusions.

Two of the girls, Gill and Kat, had very poor attendance. According to her teachers, Gill's performance in Standard Grade courses had been jeopardised by absences in S3 of up to four weeks at a time. Her RE teacher commented 'I know her fairly well. I was going to say very well but the reason I do not know her very well is that I would – if she were much in school'.

Kat, too, has had poor attendance though, when in school, her behaviour was confident and assertive. Her teachers described how she constantly claimed attention and became quite huffy when it was not immediately forthcoming. Commentators (Osler *et al.* 2002; McLaughlin, 2005) have noted that girls' responses to difficulties are 'hidden' and often result in withdrawal from participation in school, even when still maintaining a physical presence and, eventually, such non-participation could become self-exclusion or truancy. This analysis would go some way to explaining the low exclusion of girls as it is manifested in exclusion statistics – they exclude themselves rather than be formally excluded. The case study girls here were not in this group. In fact, in the view of some professionals interviewed, the girls, and others, would benefit from their strategic withdrawal from certain situations and the adoption of more low-profile personas. For example, a home/school link worker commented about Kat:

> Kat in a one-to-one situation is just ideal and she wants to please regardless of who you are and I think the teachers find that as well. Once you put her in a group setting with certain individuals, then Kat will just play up and, unfortunately, she does not know when to back down.
>
> (Home/school link worker)

There was a clear difference in the extent of girls' and boys' exclusions but no indication that girls' exclusions were for different kinds of behaviour.

Conclusion

Many of the pupils in this study had been excluded at some point for general or persistent disobedience, the largest single reason for exclusions in Scotland. Sometimes, in trying to reduce exclusions, this category of exclusion has been targeted by schools as representing the 'softer' end of a continuum of reasons why young people are excluded and therefore the area where the greatest improvement could be achieved. However, exclusions in this category can represent the outcome of a conscious and sustained challenge to the teacher's authority and evidence from some case studies demonstrated this. Andy and other boys in the whole case study sample were angry and sometimes, very aggressive, losing control of themselves when confronted with what they interpreted as disrespectful or coercive behaviour from their teachers. Other boys in this study demonstrated no loss of control; on the contrary, they demonstrated very high levels of control over themselves, other pupils in the class, even over the teacher on occasion. The referrals they received were, according to their behaviour records, for reasons of general and persistent disobedience. This cause of exclusion, therefore, may be harder to tackle than is generally supposed, for it is sometimes a reflection of a deliberately oppositional attitude to school – of agency – adopted by some boys as part of a process of negotiating their gender and class identities.

This chapter identified how the negotiation of particular kinds of identity were influenced by social class and by other factors. The complexity of the identities pursued by young people was clear. These are not apparent in the simple gender dichotomies evident in strategies to tackle boys' relatively low attainment which have neglected the alignments and 'otherings' pursued by girls and boys. Girls and boys in this study cooperated to construct gender oppositions, but they also showed how the processes of negotiating gender were cut across by other forms of identity. Some of these, such as sectarian identities, are long-standing and deep-rooted in Scottish culture. Other forms of identity are the result of the impact of social and cultural change on the identities of young working-class people, for example, the adoption of Ned identities which could be seen as a cultural dimension of social exclusion. Agency was evident in the ways in which boys and girls constructed their identities through speech, dress and other forms of behaviour. It is likely that these class cultural forms of identity would be unhelpful to young people in the wider world, as well as in school.

There were no differences apparent in the reasons for girls' and boys' exclusion, the main reason for both being general disobedience and the verbal abuse of teachers. Girls' alignment of their interests with boys and in opposition to others in school could be viewed as a way of rejecting other, more passive, feminine identities. Girls and boys were not equal in these alignments. Although girls' aggressive behaviour was sometimes admired by boys, it was also spoken of in patronising ways. Through their friendships with boys, girls gained access to public spaces and to accepted norms of behaviour which would have been hard to reach in the company of other girls alone. Girls' friendships with other girls were not considered here. Observation and interview data did not allow that dimension to be opened up in the analysis.

The next chapter will consider the relationship between exclusion and young people's engagement with and participation in schooling.

Chapter 5

Negotiating identities in school
Moving towards exclusion

> 'I was one of the brightest in my class at primary school. I still am really in most of my classes. I can do the work but I just don't do it most of the time.'

Schools are recognised as an important site for the negotiation of young people's identities. The previous chapter looked at the multifaceted nature of young people's identities; this chapter will show how identities are worked out in school settings and how certain identities are tied up with processes of inclusion and exclusion. Engagement with schooling is shown to be shaped by economic as well as cultural factors, and that these two intertwine in pupils' interactions with schooling. There were signs that from S1 onwards, case study pupils were disengaging from schooling. The links between exclusion and self-exclusion or disengagement have been recognised – sometimes as a way of understanding gendered patterns of school exclusion, as noted in the previous chapter. This chapter aims to consider the negotiation of pupils' identities in school by analysing

- how the processes of schooling impact on the case study pupils' sense of who they are, and
- what effect those negotiations have on engagement with schooling, and on exclusion, in particular.

The discussion will begin by exploring school constructions of pupil abilities. These will then be related to transitions from primary school and to the teaching and organisation of classes in secondary school. Schools, and not just pupils, are shown to be actively engaged in the negotiation of pupil identities. The focus will then turn to consider the effects of pupils' relationships in school, first with teachers and other staff and then with pupils. The final section here will discuss if and how schools encourage pupils to subscribe to the social life of the school. Some pupils' lives are shown 'in the round' to show how themes in the discussion are played out in the experience of individual pupils.

Abilities

'Ability' is a central construct for schools and its application illustrates the part played by schools in the negotiation of pupil identities, as previously noted in Chapter 3 (Broadfoot, 1996; Reay and Wiliam, 1999; Hamilton, 2002). Within the whole case study sample, teachers' comments and school reports on pupils indicated a wide range of abilities. The negotiation of ability identity is a dynamic process and this was also apparent in the data. For example, some pupils were assessed in primary school as having very high abilities but secondary school experience showed a 'falling away' of their demonstrated abilities. Pupils with high abilities, and numerous exclusions, will be discussed further on in this section but there were also pupils whose behaviour difficulties were seen as bound up with general learning difficulties and the discussion will turn first to two boys in this category.

Behaviour difficulties and learning difficulties

Official statistics (SEED, 2005) showed that pupils with Records of Needs were over-represented in exclusion statistics. One possible reason for this could be the tendency for boys, in particular, to use challenging behaviour as a diversion from their learning difficulties, thus protecting their self-worth and improving their status with the peer group (Jackson, 2002). There was some evidence of this in the case studies of Joe and Gary both of whom seemed to prefer a 'bad boy' label to a learning difficulties label.

Joe

Joe was an S2 pupil who had considerable difficulty with his behaviour in secondary school. In primary school, a Record of Needs was opened because of generalised learning difficulties. In reading, he was working at Level A, the 5–14 level normally attained by six-year-olds in P2, and it was reported that he had great difficulty in accessing the curriculum in all subjects, even where differentiation strategies were used. In S2 Joe was excluded six times for a total period of 21 days. In addition, he had a further 70 days off school, giving him an attendance rate of 62.37 per cent. His misbehaviour was almost always in class. He shouted out inappropriately and drew attention to himself. He was very disruptive of lessons. Joe reported that he 'just got badder' as he went on into first year, getting ever more punishment exercises, referrals and suspensions. The assistant headteacher (AHT) believed Joe's behaviour difficulties were closely related to his learning difficulties but, if the relationship were as simple as this suggests, Joe's behaviour would have been a problem across the curriculum. The pattern of referrals in his behaviour file showed this not to have been the case. Joe said that he liked physical education and he played a number of sports. He also liked maths and English and computing. He strongly disliked French and he had been in a great deal of trouble there. When asked what makes the difference between a subject he liked and a subject he disliked Joe immediately said it was the teachers: 'A bad teacher rattles on at you all of the time, shouts at you, tells you to shut up and all that, and a good teacher . . . I don't really know'.

In certain classes, it seems that Joe's self-worth was protected for him by the teaching strategies used – he was involved, supported and achieving. In spite of the effectiveness of some of its teaching, mainstream secondary was seen by the school as the wrong place for Joe. His parents had been asked to transfer him to a school for pupils with moderate learning difficulties but they had refused. For Joe's parents, too, the learning difficulties label was unacceptable; they had stated that they did not want him stigmatised. The capacity of parents to contribute to constructions of their child's ability varied according to social class (Reay, 1998; Vincent, 2000) and their perceptions of their own position/role within education communities (Hamilton, 2002: 601). At the time of the data gathering and in view of the difficulties he was experiencing, Joe's parents had again been asked to consider transferring him out of mainstream.

Gary

Gary did not have a Record of Needs but, like Joe, he was not doing well academically. His mother felt that Gary did 'act the clown' for others in his class:

> He's just a bit immature. There are times his mouth just runs off, you know what I mean? He's all mouth. He's not a bad boy. I know every mother will say that, you know, but he just seems to get into trouble, he gets caught out at every turn and he's not fly, you know what I mean?
> (Gary's mother)

In S2, Gary's attendance was recorded as 57.80 per cent. This included 3 periods of exclusion of 3 days, 10 days and 5 days, amounting to 18 days missed through exclusion. In addition, Gary had been absent for a further 60.5 days during that session. The behaviour which led to Gary's exclusions was observed in an English lesson. He was uninterested, inattentive, kicking underneath the table at the boy opposite and then claiming he had been kicked. He was seeking and trying to create diversions. His English teacher, Mrs T, had found Gary very tiresome:

> I would say with every kid there is a redeeming feature. With Gary it is very hard to find. It is almost as though he has switched off and he is quite pleased in a way to be going in to the bottom third year section . . . He's totally disaffected for some reason or another and I have no notion why. And, of course, it is sort of self-fulfilling because he misbehaves, gets put out and back in, he is further behind, he cannot allow himself to be seen

to ask for help, therefore he misbehaves, I complain and the whole thing starts again.

(Gary's English teacher)

Gary himself presents his relationships with others in the class as the main factor in his behaviour: 'It all depends who the teacher is or who's in my class at the same time . . . If it's the teacher, like, if they don't like me or I don't like them I kind of just annoy them'.

With both Gary and Joe, there was evidence that they were prepared to pay the price of multiple exclusions to avoid the demeaning learning difficulties label. There was also evidence that this choice was not forced upon them in all classes; both boys referred to teachers as a key factor in their behaviour. The experience of Joe and Gary raises questions about the quality and the consistency of classroom provision in secondary schools. Further questions about secondary schools are raised by the boys' experience of primary school which contrasts sharply with their secondary school experience.

Transition from primary school

For some pupils, notably less able pupils in this study, the move to secondary school signalled a significant change in their relationship to schooling. For example, Joe was not excluded at all in primary school but had been excluded eight times since coming to secondary. The AHT commented that Joe seemed to cope for the first six months in secondary school but then started to misbehave. Joe himself remembers being happy in primary school and getting into very little trouble there. Similarly, Gary had been happy throughout his seven years in primary school. He had never been excluded although he did get into trouble a couple of times for what he called 'wee stupid things'. He had been happy in primary school but by the time he was in S2, Gary's attendance was just 57.80 per cent. Gary spoke wistfully of primary school: 'It was excellent. I just loved primary school. I wish I was back there . . . I just liked all the teachers. They were nice. It was a wee calm school and excellent'.

With combined experience of 14 years in primary school, Joe and Gary had no exclusions; in secondary, they each had numerous exclusions and by S2 their attendance was little better than 50 per cent. Adolescence may bring increased pressure on boys to negotiate hegemonic masculinities and this may account for the boys' contrasting experiences of primary and secondary education. Alternatively, the reason for the difference may lie in the different ways in which primary and secondary schools are organised. Both boys cited the importance of teachers. It is possible that contact with a single teacher only in primary school, and the scope for an in-depth relationship with that person, suited both boys well.

Not all pupils who had been excluded in secondary school were nostalgic about primary school. Craig came from primary school with a record of difficult behaviour, exclusions and referrals to the local Behaviour Support Base. Craig and his brother were described by the deputy headteacher (DHT) as coming from primary school with *an absolutely horrific report*. Craig had not been allowed to stay in school at lunchtime in primary school. Craig himself felt that he had suffered in secondary school as result of the reputation he brought with him from primary school. However, on inspecting his record for S1, the DHT felt that he was doing better than anticipated. Craig, too, during an interview seemed to feel that his school experience had improved since primary school:

> Things have . . . got much, much better since I came to high school and I like high school better . . . because you get more freedom and you don't stay in one classroom the whole day and you get to know more teachers. My Guidance teacher's sound and all that . . . I like my Guidance teacher.
> (Craig)

The transition experiences of Joe and Gary and their contrast with Craig's point to two issues in primary/secondary transition. First, not all pupils experience the organisation of secondary schools as difficult. For some, secondary organisation presents a welcome breadth and diversity of experience. The second issue lies in the information passed by primary schools, or more precisely, in the reception of that information in secondary schools. Reports received from pupils' primary schools were reported as influential on secondary teachers' views of pupils but this seemed to be the case only when the report was critical, as in Craig's case where there did seem to have been some advance negative labelling. Where reports of pupils were positive but their behaviour went into sharp decline in secondary, as was the case for Joe and Gary, it was assumed by the secondary school that information about the pupil had been withheld by the primary school. An AHT commenting on Joe's record voiced the opinion that primary schools were very reluctant to contact the secondary with 'negative' information about children. This assumption may have been comforting for secondary schools as it forestalled the need for them to ask why some pupils fared so badly after their move to secondary.

The constraints placed by schools on pupils' possible social identities were illustrated in the allocation of individual pupils to ability groupings. Pupils' 'identity work' here was evident in the ways in which they supported or rejected allocations to particular groupings. While the habitus allows for individual agency, it also predisposes individuals to certain ways of behaving – 'identity work' takes place within a limited range of possibilities. Reay (2002: 224), discussing how the construction of gendered identities might be more fully comprehended, noted that a main theoretical difficulty lay in understanding the extent to which individuals are constrained by their structural contexts and how far they can build alternative identities despite their stigma. Some of the case studies, such as Joe and his family, showed how powerful schools were in limiting, rather than opening up, possibilities for pupils.

Organisation of classes by ability

Pupil's ability in particular subjects shaped teachers' perceptions of that pupil, even when the teachers knew the extent of the pupil's bad behaviour elsewhere. For example, Sam had been placed in a top maths section at the end of S2, in spite of having missed almost 25 per cent of lessons that year, mainly as a result of exclusion and he also had a poor record of completing homework. His S2 maths teacher confirmed this, explaining that Sam had challenged her expectations:

> When he came to me in S2 I was quite surprised because I had one of the top S2 classes. They are split into ability groups and I had one of the top two sections. I was surprised when he came into a top section because I used to see him only outside of (S1 teacher's) class.
>
> (Maths teacher)

His S3 maths teacher noted that Sam's placement in a top set was correct in spite of earlier impressions: 'He picks up things very quickly, I would say. When you do something new Sam picks it up'.

It was interesting to note how teacher expectations operated for pupils who had a reputation for bad behaviour. Sam was considered very able in maths and in English by those subject teachers and by the AHT with overall responsibility for S1 and S2. Sam's noted ability overcame perceptions of his challenging behaviour in some subject areas where positive views of his ability shaped teachers' perspectives. This was not the case for Charlie. He used to like maths but he indicated that he no longer did. This is reflected in what his maths teacher said about him being in a General and not a Credit class as the result of his behaviour rather than his ability:

> He is more than capable of the work. He is actually bored with the work but because he is in that class, he has to do it . . . he is the best one in the class because he should not actually be there.
>
> (Maths teacher)

Charlie had been removed from his previous class because he had sworn at the teacher. The DHT commented that his relationship with the maths teacher had been damaged irreparably and that the decision had been taken to move him into another class. Unsurprisingly, some problems with his behaviour were again materialising. Some boys welcomed the status conferred by their placement in higher ability bands, even though this might cause problems by separating them from their friendship group. For others, such placement entailed negotiations they were unwilling or unable to be involved in, for example, in their relationships with particular teachers. Identities were negotiated in such very specific contexts but they were also seen to be emerging from pupils' overall engagement with schooling.

Pedagogies

Very uneven patterns of behaviour were also evident for pupils who had low levels of attainment. There was evidence that this was related to very uneven provision across the curriculum. For example, Jim was also noted as having behaviour difficulties related to his learning difficulties. His English was recorded as Level A and his maths as Level C. Jim was observed in two lessons, music and English and interestingly, his behaviour contrasted sharply in the two lessons. In music, there were just 12 pupils present and the class was set to work individually through exercises on the keyboards using headphones and a workbook suitable for their level of ability. The teacher spent a good deal of time with Jim at the beginning of the lesson, making sure he understood what he was to do, taking him through examples and helping him to get started. In spite of this, Jim sought the teacher's attention throughout the lesson, claiming to have technical problems with the keyboard/headphones and also that he could not do the work. On each occasion, the teacher went to check out his problem, either the headphones/keyboard were found to be working or Jim demonstrated that he could, in fact, do the example. Once, another pupil, a girl, went over to help Jim to sort his headphones. By the end of the lesson Jim was at his third keyboard, although the ones he had left were both in working order. He had worked on his own for no more than two minutes at a stretch before putting his hand up to claim he needed help of one kind or another.

After the music lesson the teacher confirmed that this attention-seeking behaviour was typical of Jim. His concentration and ability to work on his own were always very limited. During an interview the music teacher commented that, up until several years previously, pupils like Jim would have been in a special school. In music, Jim was in a practical-size class of 15 maximum. From observing Jim in this lesson it was not clear if his difficulties were real, that is, related to his inability to undertake the work set, or a strategy for diverting attention away from his difficulties, or both of these.

Jim was also observed in English in a full-sized mixed-ability class of 25. As well as the teacher, the principal teacher (PT) of English was present for part of the time as a normal timetabled commitment. Jim's behaviour there was in direct contrast to the music lesson; he was quiet, attentive and fully engaged with the lesson. This was a whole class lesson with a collective discussion of a film clip to which Jim contributed very effectively and during which he seemed to be entirely focused. When a question was asked of the class as a whole, Jim raised his hand and gave the right answer for which he received considerable praise from the teacher.

What do these contrasting episodes mean for Jim, for other pupils whose measured attainment is low and for the organisation of learning and teaching? The English department in this school has a long-standing commitment to mixed-ability organisation of classes and has highly developed pedagogies and resources to facilitate more inclusive ways of working (Black-Hawkins *et al.*

2007). All English teachers cooperatively teach with each other at some point in the week. This seemed to foster a collective responsibility for pupils and ongoing discussions about teaching methods, for example, the decision to use media texts, as well as printed texts, to enable pupils with reading difficulties to participate in classroom processes. In this lesson, Jim seemed relaxed, he smiled, chatted quietly to other pupils, and engaged with the teacher by putting his hand up to volunteer answers. Jim's English teacher argued strongly that the inclusive setting of a mixed-ability class was the main factor in providing well for pupils with learning/behaviour difficulties such as Jim:

> How are they going to learn how to behave in a class if they are not there? How are they going to learn what is acceptable behaviour if they are not there? How are they going to learn to take praise? And that is such a huge thing for these boys because they do not know how to take praise – they cannot accept compliments . . . I do not know how they can do that without being in class and seeing the other kids doing the good stuff . . . seeing the other kids putting up their hands and seeing the other kids getting enthusiastic about something.
>
> (English teacher)

Jim's very contrasting experience points to the importance of classroom pedagogies in inclusion. From this little piece of evidence, class size in itself seemed not to be important – Jim fared better in a group of 25 than in a group of 12 – and mixed-ability organisation may also have been ineffective had the English Department not had very well worked out classroom strategies to ensure the participation of all pupils. A further factor may also explain Jim's contrasting experiences. The English teacher, a young and inexperienced teacher, and the PT English both articulated a strong commitment to inclusive schools and inclusive classes, unlike the music teacher who felt that Jim should not have been in mainstream school. The value position of teachers came across as a crucial factor shaping attitudes to pupils and capacity to provide well for them. They were able to combine effective pedagogies with a wider commitment to social justice in education (Florian and Rouse, 2001; Florian and Kershner, 2009).

'Bright' boys

Some pupils had high levels of general ability and, sometimes, particular ability in traditional 'male' subjects such as mathematics and physics. One behaviour support teacher saw this as a departure from her early teaching experience:

> And I, I mean I'm not really too sure, and I would say, and it's not even just now that our boys are poor ability, because I would even have said,

that in the past it used to be kids that struggled with the curriculum. The curriculum was a huge barrier.

Ross, one of the case studies discussed in Chapter 4, was noted by all teachers as a very able boy. His abilities were demonstrated not just in traditional measures of attainment but in his social interactions. He did well in primary school and, on transfer to secondary, he was working within the 5–14 curriculum at Level E in maths, that is, well beyond the normal range of attainment for children of his age. In spite of very poor attendance and exclusion, he was still in the top maths section in secondary school. Ross aspired to a powerful and high-status masculinity and he seemed to be sustaining this identity in school. He was treated by other boys with a mixture of admiration and deference. There was a sense of his life taking on a very different orientation:

> He is a very bright boy but he is out till 1.00 or 2.00 a.m. and he cannot get up in the morning for school. He has a difficult home life but there is a lot of pressure as well with peers.
>
> (Home/school link worker)

School seemed to be diminishing in importance for Ross but his recognised ability was still a point of pride with him: 'I was one of the brightest in my class at primary school. I still am really in most of my classes. I can do the work; but I just don't do it most of the time'.

It is possible that, in turning away from school, Ross was making a choice, similar to that made by Willis' 'lads'. The identity he was seeking to negotiate – or needed to negotiate – could not be achieved in a school setting. Agency in pupils' exclusion will be pursued further on but before that, the experience of Davy will be introduced. Like Ross he was acknowledged as bright and he had been excluded but by S3 he seemed to be making choices quite different from Ross's.

Davy

Davy was keen to portray himself as a boy's boy, emphasising that he had a lot of friends and a girlfriend. Davy had had two exclusions, both of them during the previous year when he had been in S2. Davy's exclusions had been for bringing a knife into school and for aggressive and threatening behaviour towards a girl. Both exclusion incidents had involved other boys and there seemed to have been some bravado on Davy's part on both occasions. The knife incident had come to light when a local woman had phoned the school to report that she had seen several of its pupils with a knife at the bus stop that morning. Davy emerged as the one who had brought the knife into school. The second exclusion arose when a girl saw Davy with her friend's stolen mobile phone. Davy had bought the phone not realising that it had been stolen. He subsequently threatened the girl in the corridor and was excluded for this bullying behaviour towards her.

For a bright working-class boy like Davy, university was not on the horizon at all. He cited his intention of 'staying on' to the post-compulsory period but his view of schooling was highly instrumental. He presented the 'S' Grades and Highers he hoped to achieve as a passport to a better job, a means of achieving a higher standard of living in the future. It may have been that this was one way for Davy to square his academic aspirations with the values of his friendship group. Although university could also be said to provide a better standard of living in the future, the boys had no evidence of that within their own social sphere. Davy's emphasis on schooling as a means for him to earn more money may indicate that working-class boys grow up more quickly than their middle-class counterparts. At just 14, Davy saw himself in a settled relationship with a girl and as having to make plans about how he would earn a living. For him, the reasons for not going to university stacked up: university would be a socially unknown experience; its potential benefits were unproven; it required one to remain in education until the age of 22 – a timescale quite out of keeping with how working-class boys saw their lives progressing; and, more recently, the financial resources required for participation in higher education would be unavailable to him. Also motivating against the boys' participation in higher education was their sense of being 'anchored' to their own social, cultural and geographical base and of their need to construct a future for themselves within that sphere. Coming through strongly from the case study boys was their sense of belonging to a particular place but this could also be a metaphor for cultural affiliation and the threat of dislocation posed by academic success. Commentators (Epstein, 1997) have noted the experience of working-class students who articulated their sense of 'leaving' and 'holding on' to their culture as they entered middle-class higher education institutions.

The notion of the education system as meritocratic is challenged by data in this study. A number of the case study pupils had been judged as very able in primary school and their abilities continued to be recognised by their teachers in secondary school, even though their attainment was falling in relation to their peers. Sometimes, this happened through the agency of pupils as they started to make decisions about their future lives in relation to their present circumstances. Family attitudes were the crucial factor in how boys' saw schooling with regard to their future lives, with some boys prepared to move away from their peer group to pursue academic success. Families were key in the class cultural reproductions of pupils in this study but schools, too, were actively engaged in those processes.

For some pupils, continued engagement with schooling was sustained by positive relationships in the school setting. The next section will examine how relationships with staff impacted on pupils.

Relationships with staff

One of the striking things about some of the case study data was the very different perspectives offered by different adults about the same pupil. Chapter 4 touched upon this when discussing Gill whose business studies teacher described herself as absolutely mystified by the school's decision to exclude Gill. This section explores these differences, tries to account for them and associates them with levels of pupil engagement.

It was noted previously that teachers' perceptions of pupil ability overcame reservations about their challenging behaviour and allowed a space to be created for the pupil, for example, in a top set, where they could perform well. Sometimes pupils formed key relationships with particular teachers on the basis of personal affinity or, more surprisingly, shared academic interests. Again, it was interesting how a pupil's ability in a subject shaped teachers' perceptions of that pupil, even when the teachers knew the extent of the pupil's bad behaviour elsewhere. Jack provided an example of a pupil who was almost completely disengaged with mainstream schooling but who retained one positive point of contact.

Jack

Jack was described by the DHT as 'very bright and very angry'. He was very self-assured and articulate during an interview. He had already started to earn a living, working in a chip van two nights a week from 4.00–10.00 p.m. For these 12 hours he earned £30.00. He had been excluded many times, starting in primary school and always for angry outbursts. He was reported as being very confrontational with teachers, refusing to cooperate and then becoming abusive when he was pressured. One referral described how he was asked to stand outside the classroom because of an outburst he had had. When the teacher came to speak to him he called him *a f***ing bastard, f***ing black jake, f***ing poof.* This resulted in one of his exclusions. He attended an off-site behaviour support base for 2 × 0.5 days per week. When in school, therefore, he was on a part-time timetable. The home/school link worker had had input and there was liaison with the Social Work Department.

There was wide agreement that Jack was very able and that, had his life been different, he would be going to university. The headteacher, who had not been nominated as one of the interviewees for this research, took time to come to offer comment about Jack, 'Of all our pupils, Jack is the one I fear most for – so bright but how he copes with the circumstances in which he is living I do not know'.

The influence of wider circumstances on pupils' participation in schooling, and their exclusion, will be discussed in the next chapter but schools sometimes offered pupils a positive connection even when the pupil was moving quickly away from schooling. Jack's abilities lay in the area of mathematics and physics and his physics teacher described him as gifted. Although Jack had been excluded on numerous occasions since primary school, this teacher had never had a problem with him. The physics teacher attributed this to a mutually respectful relationship. He had found that Jack responded well to positive feedback:

> If you push Jack too hard you get a bad reaction. If you encourage him, he tends to go with you. He likes, not direct compliments, but reminders that he is good. He likes reminders that he is good, he is quality.
>
> (Physics teacher)

Although Jack's frequent non-attendance had repercussions for the continuous assessment components of his Standard Grade courses, Jack was nevertheless expected to do very well. It was unlikely that the strong and mutually respectful relationship with his physics teacher would be enough to keep Jack within the school system once he reached the school-leaving age at 16. As reported previously, Scottish Executive Education Department (SEED) guidelines on exclusions (SEED, 2003) were changed to ensure that exclusion from school was not exclusion from education. Pupils excluded for more than three days had to have schoolwork provided. Although this stipulation was welcomed by local authority (LA) staff, in schools it was viewed as tokenism in that teachers would be unable to supply a distance education pack customised for pupils and that, even where such material could be provided, excluded pupils would be unlikely to complete the work at home for a range of reasons. The intention to maintain continuity in pupils' education could be applauded when considering the experience of Jack. As previously noted, he had high abilities in maths and physics but was also very angry and capable of very aggressive behaviour. The school system does not cope well with this combination of intellectual giftedness and very challenging behaviour. Always, the behaviour becomes the main focus for attention. Jack had had six exclusions during S3, one of them for three weeks. In all, he had missed 37 school days in S3 because of exclusion. His overall attendance record was 67.75 per cent, though some of that attendance has been at a behaviour support base where he would not follow a normal curriculum but would focus on Personal and Social Development in areas such as anger management. The amount of time he had out of the ordinary curriculum had an impact on his educational attainment. Jack's physics teacher had never had a problem with Jack in his class and was therefore aggrieved that Jack's exclusions had undermined his performance in physics. 'His last non-attendance was due to the school deeming him not to be suitable in my class' (Physics teacher).

Jack's physics teacher argued that it would be important from a societal point of view to get Jack into an apprenticeship of some kind and away from possibly a very violent life on the streets. He felt that withdrawing him from academic subjects where he excelled was not the way to support his future. There is a common dilemma here for schools in the strategies they use to support pupils with challenging behaviour. Behaviour support bases whether in school or off campus, have gone some way to providing the kind of flexibility schools needed in managing the very challenging behaviour of some pupils. Bases are very different in their aims and functioning (Head *et al.* 2003; Kane *et al.* 2004). All offer a form of 'internal exclusion' (Munn *et al.* 2000), serving a dual function, that is, keeping pupils off the streets and off the school's exclusion statistics. However, while some bases are 'sin bins' aiming for containment only, other bases offer a more developed educational provision. Even where provision in bases is purposeful and helpful to pupils, though, it cannot replicate the depth and breadth of the ordinary curriculum. Thus, the flexibility bases offered by schools in their organisation is something very different in terms of the curriculum experience of pupils. Jack's physics teacher says he would be delighted to teach physics to Jack six times a week and he feels that the system should be flexible enough to allow for this. He argued that education should take different forms so that exclusion from ordinary school should never be exclusion from education. He argued strongly for multiple solutions to the problem of bad behaviour and exclusions to accommodate the wide range of pupils affected. It was hoped, though, that the recognition Jack had received about his mathematical ability would encourage him one day to return to education.

Sometimes, a key positive relationship in the school was a pupil's relationship with a member of staff who was not a teacher. Government funding had enabled the establishment of new posts, home/school link workers, as they were called in this LA. Comments coming through in pupil interviews were testament to the effectiveness of those staff in forming relationships with pupils who were otherwise hard to reach. For example,

> like, there's Rab. See people like who have been referred to him, and you go to his club on a Monday after school. He's good but he tells you he's not your social worker, he's not your teacher, he's your pal. That's quite good cos you can listen to him. He's not trying to shout at you, he's not trying to get a pure bad point across to you, he's just talking away to you and he gets to know you and that. He's good . . . He's only in his early thirties. If you got more of them in the school I think that would be better.
>
> (Ross, S1)

Sometimes, difficulties in relationships between pupils and teachers seemed to lie in pupils' limited social skills. For example, Baz's RE teacher had known him very well throughout S1 and S2. This teacher saw some of Baz's difficulties as lying in an inability to gauge the appropriateness of his behaviour towards teachers:

> Baz is a very sincere young man. He has a heart of gold. I think he has a strange relationship with some teachers. He is a friendly young man and

he wants to be friendly. I think he has a great sense of humour as well but he does not know the barriers of the relationship between pupil and teacher . . . and I think what he tends to do is to overstep the mark slightly. It is not always obvious how he oversteps the mark but he does.

(RE teacher)

This is an interesting point in that Baz and some of his friends may have only one way of conducting positive relationships with other men and that way may be quite incompatible with the deference expected in pupil relationships with teachers. It might be that Baz has not learned the subtleties involved in maintaining different kinds of social relationships.

Similarly, one of the case study girls, Gill, had sometimes fraught relationships with teachers arising from the manner and tone of her interactions with them. She was noted as claiming a parity of status that was unacceptable to staff:

. . . you have to say to her, 'That's not how you should speak to a teacher.' . . . Her justification was that's how she speaks to her mum and her mum is more important than anyone.

(History teacher)

'Respect' came through strongly as an issue for both teachers and pupils but, clearly, there were differences in interpreting behaviour as disrespectful or not. Pupils may or may not have intended attitudes or behaviours to be disrespectful to teachers and, among staff groups within the same schools, there were different views of what constituted 'respectful' behaviour. Some of these differences related to teachers' notions of authority and it is possible that what they sought from pupils was deference and not respect. This would be culturally very challenging for some of the boys in this study. It was notable that the home/school link workers interviewed had strong relationships with the pupils they dealt with and seemed to accept much more informality in their relationships with pupils, for example pupils called them by their first names. Some of these relationships with boys were characterised by mutual respect. The next section will consider pupil relationships within the peer group.

Peers, friends and social networks

This section aims to consider the place of relationships among pupils as a means of fostering case study pupils' connectedness to schooling. A main attraction of school for many of the case study pupils, and especially the boys, was the facility offered to socialise with peers. There were indications that masculine identities were developed within the peer group individually and also collectively as a response to what Willis (1978) has called the 'unjustified authority' exerted over them by school. A number of pupils indicated that the really negative impact of exclusion was that it closed down for them an important social forum. Commentators have identified the influence of the peer group on adolescent boys as a significant factor in their conflict with the institutional authority of the school (Connell, 1989: 291; Mac an Ghaill, 1994). Boys in this study endorsed strongly the importance of friends to them, commenting, for example: *Friends are always there beside you right through life.* It was also clear that boys' friendship groups exerted very strong influence upon them and one which was demonstrated in lessons in which case study boys were participating.

In a Personal and Social Education lesson observed, the impact of Davy's social group on his behaviour was very apparent. Davy sat with a group of ten boys whose dress was a kind of uniform within the school uniform and distinguished them from others in the class. This group operated quite consciously as a group, teasing each other and encouraging each other to annoy others in the class, especially girls. Davy was in the thick of the group and was very involved in attempting to attract the attention of a girl sitting in front of him. The boys participated in the lesson but, to a much greater extent, they were engaging with their own friendship group. Once the teacher put on a video, the boys moved to sit on the desks, still keeping close to each other. They maintained their conversation, which was about drugs and the video itself, throughout the film. The rest of the class – all of the girls and a few boys – were quiet and attentive throughout. This episode was a very vivid illustration of how his friendship group had an impact on Davy. He was very much part of a group of mates who were prepared to participate in the lesson but very largely on their own terms.

Mac an Ghaill (1994: 56) noted that for the boys in his study, the peer group provided the 'significant others' in the school setting, offering continuing feedback and guidance as to proper attitudes to schooling and future lives. There was considerable evidence in this study coming from pupils and teachers of peer group influence as a factor in boys' challenging behaviour and exclusion from school:

> I think some of it, with the difficult boys we have in here, there is a peer thing goes on there. I don't think there is any doubt that Andy likes to entertain the other boys in the class. I think he also likes to entertain the girls, but he doesn't do it an obvious way. It's always a boy he connects with . . . And I think a big part of it, for the majority of them is, they already have a reputation. And what they do is they continue to live that reputation.
>
> (Principal teacher behaviour support)

Boys themselves discussed how the trouble they got into in school and out-of-school was related to their friendship group. Charlie recounted how in P6 he had 'started getting bolder and started getting in with the wrong crowd'. He and his friends had been in trouble out in the community. Baz, too, recounted how some of the difficulties he had been in were caused by his efforts to perform for his friends. Baz has been excluded twice in S2. The first time was for five days for maliciously setting off the fire alarm. Baz indicated that he had been incited by his friends:

> The fire strike was on and people were going to set off the fire bell. Somebody asked me to do it . . . and I felt, 'Oh, I could do this and I could really be something big if I done this'. So I was the one that done it.

Sometimes pupils were excluded because of their intervention in incidents which did not concern them. For example, the DHT recounted how Andy had stormed off having been in trouble in detention. He walked across the playground at lunchtime calling back to the DHT and another teacher, 'You are a pair of dafties. Your school stinks. It is a dump'. The verbal abuse continued as he walked across the playground to the school gate. Other pupils, some of whom were his friends, observing this, called on him to come back and not to be so daft but Andy continued on his way. Then Craig realised what had happened and approached the DHT insisting that his brother could not be sent home in this way. 'What have you done to my brother? You can't send him home. Get him a taxi' (Craig). The DHT explained that Andy was going home of his own free will and would not be getting a taxi. Craig then turned away saying to the DHT, 'F**k off'. He was then excluded himself.

Boys' friendships could and did have negative effects for their schooling but they also brought a number of advantages. First, these friendships offered closeness and continuity. The friendships seemed to be very stable and enduring. Some of Charlie's friendships had lasted since P1 and he envisaged that they would be lifelong. Eddie, too, commented: 'me and S— have been friends since primary school and all that. Like, when my Ma and Da went on holiday and I was too young to go, his Ma watched me and that'.

Second, friendships offered solidarity and therefore protection to boys. Aggression featured largely in some boys' accounts of enmity and friendship. Competence at fighting was highly regarded among friendship groups. One or two boys explained that friendships came about because friends were able to stand up for you when you were being bullied. There was then an obligation to do the same for them. There seemed to be a very strong code of honour operating where it was expected that you should accept blame, even when you were innocent, if it spared your pal. One or two boys reported that they had been excluded for things done by pals but that this was acceptable to them. The third advantage of boys' friendships was that they provided 'good fun'. Humour was very important to the boys interviewed and considerable status was accorded to boys who could make others laugh.

How do schools deal with boys' friendships when they are frequently a basis for oppositional attitudes to schooling? Sometimes, the setting or streaming of classes is a means of splitting up friendship groups in S3. When pupils enter edStandard Grade courses, and sometimes earlier than that, classes were organised on the basis of ability. Although there was evidence from this study and elsewhere that the disproportionate number of boys allocated to bottom sets is a reflection of motivation, rather than ability. For example, Charlie, whose placing in a low maths set was discussed previously, indicated that he used to like maths but that he no longer did. His maths teacher confirmed that he was in a General class rather than a Credit class as the result of his behaviour rather than his ability. Charlie had made a choice to continue to challenge teachers in order to maintain his status with his peer group.

However, for one or two of the case study boys, 'ability' sets allowed some space for them to move away from their friendship group. Davy was at a crossroads in his life. He had been and continued to be one of the lads, behaving in and out of the classroom in ways that got him into trouble along with his mates. However, his academic aspirations were taking him away from those mates. For a number of subjects, Davy was finding himself in different sections from his friends. One of his teachers reported that he 'showed ability early on but he did not play to his strength. He tried not to show that he was clever because it was not cool within that class' (English teacher). Going into S3, Davy was placed in a top Credit class for English and his teacher thought that he might resent being separated from his friends. When she asked Davy about this privately, she discovered that he was pleased to be in this class. He had been doing very well, bringing homework to her on a one-to-one basis to check it with her.

The majority of the case study boys rated friendship very highly in their lives and many of them showed that friendship had played a direct or an indirect part in their exclusion. This was not the case for all of the boys here. Ewen was a notable exception. He was the only case study pupil to come from a middle-class and affluent background. He had no friends in the school, although some of his exclusions seemed to be as a result of giving cheek to teachers in an effort to gain peer approval. The behaviour support teacher reported that Ewen's parents tried to engineer friendships for him, sometimes picking out boys and suggesting that they would make suitable friends. Ewen's parents took him to a middle-class suburb some distance away so he could take part in a rugby club there. The young men he associated with there were in their twenties. Coming across strongly from Ewen during an interview was his sense of isolation from other boys and his awareness of difference from them. He acknowledged his social advantage – he mentioned his dad's laptop – and he had identified that, unlike him, most boys who were excluded 'came from bad areas'.

Different from the majority of case study boys was Jack. He seemed to get on well enough with other pupils he had no real friendships in school and, unlike Ewen, he did not seek friendships. He was described as a loner, as assuming that when he left the class he had no contact with any of the other pupils. This is attributed to his maturity and to his being very worldly wise and therefore finding very little in the company of other young people of his age. It is also possible that significant family responsibilities, such as shopping and caring for younger siblings, and his job, prevented Jack having the time or the resources to maintain friendships. When asked for his analysis of the gender imbalance in exclusions, Jack reported that he knew girls who were just like him – that is, with significant family cares and responsibilities – except they were never in school to get into trouble.

Does the peer group exert the same influence on girls in relation to exclusions? This study has not been informed by the experience of a broad and diverse group of girls since its scope was formal exclusion from school. However, the girls in this study were unlike those most often identified in the literature. While in school, they were reported as having friends, being popular, even. Classroom observation similarly showed the girls to be socially well-integrated with their peer group. To that extent, the excluded girls had much in common with the majority of the excluded boys. Interviews with most of the case study pupils, girls and boys, indicated that they saw their friendship group as encompassing both genders. The existence of cross-gender friendships came across strongly in interviews and they were often cited with pride. It seemed to be important to these young adolescents that they had male and female friends, in addition to the romantic/sexual relationships which some of them also mentioned.

Case study pupils, girls and boys, found that school offered an important site for creating and maintaining friendship groups. Those friendships could operate in opposition to schools. For many boys masculine identities were developed within the peer group and as part of a collective response to the school's differentiated forms of authority. The boys in this study had that in common with Willis' lads. Unlike Willis' lads, their post-school transitions would not be experienced collectively. The final section of this chapter will look at case study pupils' participation in the broad community of their schools beyond the curriculum.

Joining in

All four secondary schools in this study operated a range of extra-curricular activities in, for example, sport, music and drama. Pupils in the case study sample had very low rates of participation here unsurprisingly, perhaps, when many of them had very poor attendance rates. There are issues here related to the economic and cultural resources of pupils' families. For example, Andy who was 12 years old, indicated that he had given up playing football on a Saturday morning because he could not get himself out of bed in time for the match. The themes of poverty and family and their effect on children's engagement with schooling will be picked up further in the next chapter. There were some attempts on the part of schools to encourage pupils' participation beyond the formal curriculum as a means of enhancing their overall engagement with schooling. Baz provides one such example.

Baz

Baz was popular and was at the centre of a group of boys who were good friends. Baz and many of his friends had been in trouble of various kinds in school. Because the trouble Baz had been involved in had not usually been in the classroom, he had not been on a behaviour monitoring sheet. This meant that he was seen in quite a positive light by many of his teachers who felt they had a good relationship with him. The DHT desbribed Baz as *a Jack-the-lad, quite a happy-go-lucky boy and, actually, quite a likeable lad.* Baz's file from primary school indicated a similar pattern of behaviour and relationships. It was noted in his primary school report that other pupils sought his approval. He had been made a House captain but had it removed from him. During an interview, Baz spoke a good deal about his pride in this:

> Well, I put my name down to be the Captain or the Vice-captain but I did not think I would get it . . . other people in the House would pick who it was. And there's a boy, Martin Lee, got picked for the House Captain and I thought, 'Oh, no. I have not got a chance any more. Then I was well happy when my name came out for Vice'.

It was not clear if the process of selecting the Captain and Vice-captain was genuinely democratic. It is possible that the school wished to make Baz more of a stakeholder in the school by giving him a measure of responsibility. If so, this tactic seemed to work according to Baz's own account:

> People were looking up to you and a lot of people would come to you if they needed help, like the wee ones, I mean. They would all ask you for some help and that so you felt a lot more authority. You felt as if maybe you had done well for yourself and that you were higher up, like close to your mum and that.
>
> (Baz)

Many of the case study pupils showed a range of abilities and skills, including well-developed social skills and high levels of self-awareness. Almost all of the case study pupils were on the margins of school life. For some of them, that was because the margins were where they chose to be. Other influences in their lives mattered more than school. For other pupils, though, and especially those in S1, a more interventionist approach which promoted their involvement in social and recreational activity might have strengthened their connection to schooling.

Conclusion

This chapter set out to consider the negotiation of pupils' identities in school by analysing how the processes of schooling impacted on the case study pupils' identities and by considering the effect of those negotiations on engagement with schooling, and on exclusion, in particular. Ability, and being seen to have it, mattered a great deal to the case study sample. Even boys who no longer cared about doing well in school valued the 'very bright' label. One of the main ways in which schooling influenced identity negotiation was through its power to attribute and withhold ability labels such as 'bright' and 'learning difficulties'. Pupils' behaviour was central to schools' negotiations here with decisions about placement in particular classes, or even special schools, made on the basis of behaviour and not ability. Schools did not see their manipulation of ability identities as a means of controlling pupil behaviour but some pupils experienced it as such and reacted by becoming further distanced from schooling.

Particular problems for secondary schools emerged. Some case study pupils reacted badly to the more fragmented curriculum organisation of secondary school with its compartmentalised subjects and range of teachers. They seemed not to have found the means of connecting to secondary as they had with primary. This may have related to the lack of an ongoing positive relationship with a single, or main, teacher. Pupils certainly articulated the view that it was teachers who made the difference for them but there was evidence that it was teaching, too, that made a difference. Some lessons observed were carefully planned to ensure the participation of all pupils and they succeeded in this aim. Other lessons had an alienating effect on pupils. If pupil identities are shaped by pupils' internalisation of school and teacher criteria, there was evidence of schools shaping pupil identities in ways that were ultimately very challenging for the school.

Teachers' values, as well as their professional skills and commitments, made a difference to pupil experience. Their attitudes to pupils were central in determining how pupils responded to them. Again and again, pupils spoke of 'respect' and of the lack of it as a reason for their insolence, disobedience and, sometimes, total loss of control. This was partly to do with teachers' views that they had to maintain authority, implying that pupils should not talk back or question them, but there may be other factors at work here for some teachers seemed able to maintain authority alongside respectful relationships with pupils. There was wide variation in the relationships case study pupils enjoyed with their teachers, with some very sharp contrasts. Sometimes ability in a particular subject allowed a bond between the teacher of that subject and the pupil; in other cases, teachers seemed to see something to be liked and/or respected in the pupil allowing a positive relationship to develop. Whatever the basis of these relationships, they gave pupils a valuable link to schooling when they were otherwise very alienated. More could perhaps be made of these links by allowing pupils more time in those areas of the curriculum, or with those teachers.

Schools were an important social site for pupils and their identities were shaped in and by the peer group which spanned school and pupils' broader experience. The next chapter will discuss exclusions and the wider social context, beginning with family.

Chapter 6

Exclusion and young people's lives

> 'I know for me I don't think. I just take life as it comes . . . you don't know if you are going to be here in four year's time so why not just live for the moment? Because you don't know if your family . . . and you don't know if you are going to be there.'

The previous chapter considered the part played by schools in the negotiation of case study pupils' identities, and the inclusionary and exclusionary effects of school processes. This chapter looks at broader aspects of case study pupils' lives and considers the impact of those factors on their exclusion from school. Policy was criticised in Chapter 2 for its over-emphasis of school improvement as a means of tackling challenging behaviour and exclusion. Case study data will be used here to illustrate the shortcomings of that policy. Discussion will address if and how the wider circumstances of pupils' lives contribute towards their exclusion from school. Some factors have already been highlighted, for example, case study pupils' sense of belonging to a particular locality was shown to be formative of their identities. Themes to be considered here are:

- Families and exclusions
- Poverty
- Aggression and violence
- Future lives

In relating these themes to exclusion from school, the question of agency will again arise. Are excluded pupils turning away from school and, if so, to what extent are they exercising choice?

Families and exclusions

Exclusions could create further pressure on fraught family relationships. One indication of this was the difficulty experienced in trying to gain parents' participation in this study. Several parents consented to be interviewed but subsequently withdrew. This may have been because of embarrassment at their children having been excluded but there were also indications that arrangements were sometimes hard for parents to follow through; several interviews were cancelled at short notice.

Professional key informants had justified exclusion primarily as a signal to pupils and their families that certain behaviour was unacceptable. Where families were very responsive to school concerns, the exclusion itself could be averted. For the mothers of some case study pupils, exclusion, or the threat of exclusion, could not serve this purpose for they had no capacity to respond in ways that might change the situation in school. In most cases, pupils returning from exclusion and his/her parents are asked to give a guarantee of future good behaviour, sometimes even signing a contract to that effect as a condition of the pupil's re-admission. This mechanism assumes a measure of parental control which in some cases is entirely ill-founded. Similarly, some recent policy ideas have suggested that parents be made more accountable for their children's behaviour by, for example, fining parents when children transgress. This is misguided in its assumption that all parents are able to exercise control over their children and would simply increase pressure on families whose situation is already precarious.

Exclusion did operate as a punishment to pupils and to their families. This purpose of exclusion was not acknowledged by local and national officials. From some case study pupils' accounts, it was difficult to separate out the impact of exclusions on them from the impact on their families; such was the upset caused to families and the repercussions to pupils from that source. For Baz, exclusion was very clearly a punishment: He described himself as feeling:

> like a failure, as if I had really, really, really let myself and my family down. And I thought that I had let good friends down as well because they did not expect it of me and that. I did not feel too good when it all happened.

A further impact of exclusions was on Baz's relationship with his mother. He seemed to have a very caring attitude towards her and described how upset she was, particularly when he was excluded for a second time:

> Well, my mum thought it would just be a one-off, then about two months later, that [a further exclusion] happened. My mum considered getting me to see somebody to see if there was, like, something up with me and that. My family had all split up and it would probably have been something to do with that.

Baz is here referring to his parents' acrimonious separation and to his mother' fears that Baz's unacceptable behaviour was a reaction to losing contact with his father. She had asked, and the school had considered, referring Baz to the educational psychologist. For Baz and his family, his exclusion was a punishment, causing a great deal of stress to family relationships.

Similarly, Ewen reported that his family got very upset by the difficulties he had in school. In relation to his exclusion, he said 'I dread telling my mum because I know how much my mum is upset . . . She cries a lot with me. She tells my Grans and my Grans are really worried and that'.

When Ewen is excluded, his family back up the punishment as he has to stay in his room and get on with schoolwork. Ewen reported that his exclusions were taken very seriously by his family:

> Well, my dad sits us down and says, 'Look, what do we have to do with you?' and sometimes I get hit or something and I get shouted at or grounded and I have to go up to my room.
>
> (Ewen)

Exclusion was a punishment for Ewen because of his family's reaction. In spite of this, there was no deterrent effect. Ewen was excluded again and again. Support systems in schools have developed in recent years so that pupils in trouble can review their behaviour and try to learn new ways of managing their reactions and their conflict with others. For some pupils like Ewen, the changes needed to avoid further exclusion were beyond them. They seemed locked into a cycle of unacceptable behaviour followed by exclusion, ending in their permanent exclusion and removal from the register of the school.

By contrast, Maz is one of the 61 per cent of pupils in Scotland who had just one exclusion from school and that was for only five days. The exclusion and the incident which caused it seem to have had a very heavy impact on Maz. He consented to be interviewed but during the interview he was clearly very embarrassed about it, saying that he did not wish to tell me what had happened. Nor did he wish me to interview his mother although she had already formally signalled her consent to be interviewed. Not all pupils saw exclusion as a punishment. Within the case study sample, all girls and most boys experienced exclusion as a punishment but an exception was Gary: 'I feel quite glad because it's like a holiday to me because I still get to go out and play on my bike or whatever'.

Parental attitudes were a key factor in whether or not exclusions were experienced as a punishment or a deterrent. Some parents were unable to back up the school's punishment. They lacked the physical and personal resources that might have made this possible. Gary's mother said that they had attempted to keep Gary in his room without his computer and television during his exclusions but they had found this very difficult to sustain over say, a period of ten days. Gary was able, therefore, to meet with his friends even when he was excluded from school:

> See when I was suspended, I went down to the chip shop, down at the shops at lunchtime and I met them all down there and I got something to eat and all that and then we went back up to my house.
>
> (Gary)

However, Gary was not allowed to attend football training when he was suspended and he conceded that this was a loss to him. Although Gary's mother accepted that his behaviour was a problem for the school, she was adamant that exclusions served no useful purpose. She advocated some kind of restorative approach to unacceptable behaviour:

> I think children in general like exclusion from school. They are quite happy to be sent home. I mean, I think it's defeating the purpose sending them home. I think the best thing to do – if they break something around the school, get them to fix it in school, help the janitor, do something in school – you know what I mean?
>
> (Gary's mother)

Rising exclusions had prompted concern about the vulnerability of children to involvement in crime and other antisocial activity when they were out of school, and about a possible increase in crime suffered by the community when numbers of children were unsupervised. For exclusions to have a positive or even a neutral effect, on pupils and on the wider community, the active cooperation of parents is required. Many parents in this study lacked the means needed to support schools' action in excluding their child.

More worrying, the impact of exclusion on families could be long term, colouring parents' attitudes towards school. Speaking of the impact her son's exclusion had on her, Gary's mother said that she became scared to go to parents' meetings: 'I was really thinking twice about going to the Parents' Night but, once I got by that, I saw that 95 per cent of the teachers were fantastic . . . It was great. I was glad I went, but I didn't want to go'.

School professionals interviewed did not mention the impact of exclusion on families' overall engagement with schooling, although this aspect came through strongly from pupils and their parents. A mismatch was apparent between schools' perceptions of parents' attitudes and the evidence available of those attitudes. Teachers seemed not to be aware of the impact their comments and actions had, nor of their power to alienate and engage. For example, Sam had been in trouble in maths for failing to complete homework and bring books back in. The maths teacher had written home on several occasions to complain about both of these problems and there had usually been an improvement after these letters. The maths teacher had never been able to talk to Sam's parents at a parents' meeting:

> They did not come to Parents' Nights and Sam was probably one of only two or three in the class whose parents I would have liked to have spoken to. Not about the behaviour, just about the homework, but they just didn't come.
>
> (Maths teacher)

An assumption from teachers that some parents were uninterested was sometimes apparent – 'did not want to know'. From the parents who were interviewed for this research, this assumption was entirely unsubstantiated. In spite of their children's exclusion, parents in general were highly sensitised to feedback from schools. Gary's mother had each night taken to copying out carefully all teachers' comments on Gary's daily behaviour monitoring card. She retained these transcribed comments as a way of reassuring herself and her son that there were many positive remarks as well as negative ones. Social inclusion policy constructed education as a way of enabling mainstream participation. School exclusions had the opposite, alienating effect.

Bourdieu's concepts of habitus, field and capitals have been used to analyse differential relationships to schooling of working-class and middle-class parents (Reay, 1998; Vincent, 2000). Those relationships are also gendered, with mothers not only responsible for maintaining home/school relationships but also mediating the lesser involvement of fathers (Reay, 1998). Class-based differences rest upon the extent to which parents can mobilise their social and cultural capitals in their engagement with their children's schools. For example, middle-class parents have access to teachers through informal social networks, knowledge of the education system and confidence in drawing upon that knowledge. They can bring to the field of education *habituses shaped by educational success and a sense of entitlement* (Reay 1998: 145). In study after study, working-class parents have been shown to be just as prepared to engage with their children's schools but lacked confidence in helping their children and were much more inclined to accept teachers' professional judgements (Reay, 1998; Vincent, 2000; Hamilton, 2002).

An interesting construction of social class and exclusions was offered by the headteacher of one of the four secondary schools. He believed that the relationship between poverty and school exclusion was not a straightforward causal one. Where the values of the family included trust in the school, it was very unlikely that the possibility of exclusion would ever arise. Some families generally seemed to deal with conflict by becoming very aggressive, shouting and so on. The headteacher reported that he had often had parents shouting down the phone at him, while the pupil stood beside the parent and heard the exchange. This lack of respect and a tendency to opt for confrontation both limited the school's options and the exclusion of the pupil would then be the only way of proceeding. The headteacher believed there was an inverse relationship between the number of exclusions experienced by a pupil and the level of support the family exhibited towards the school; some parents saw good parenting as siding with the child against the school. The headteacher's account was very reasonable in the terms in which it was explained but if 'trust in the school' means understanding how the school works, then it is clear that parents without those kinds of social and cultural capitals are unable to manage situations potentially leading to exclusion. There is also in his account a sense in which parents in that position know their disadvantage, are frustrated by it and retreat into wary defensiveness of their child. Home/school link workers have been seen as helpful in this respect, acting as advocates and mediators for parents.

There were gender differences in girls' and boys' relationships with their families. Although there were just three case study girls, all three were reported as having very strong and influential relationships with their mothers. Commentators have noted the pull of home for girls in particular, noting how often girls' non-participation in schooling culminated in withdrawal to the home, in contrast with boys (Osler and Vincent, 2003; Ridge, 2005). There was some evidence that case study girls' poor attendance, though no worse than boys', might have been for different reasons in that, for girls, there was more of a pull to be at home. The social isolation of some girls, then, would be a matter for concern, reflecting in some cases the experience of women such as Kat's mother who was described by the family support worker as withdrawn and hard to pin down for appointments and other social and support arrangements:

> We have . . . the Family Centre . . . and she [Kat's mum] could go down there and go on the different courses, stress busters and different things like that. But she is not strong enough, you know, her self-esteem is not at that level yet that she would be confident to be able to do that. But, I mean, she gets by, you know, she visits her mum and different things like that . . . she is not in the house all the time. She does get out.
>
> (Family support worker)

Sometimes, there were indications that girls' own well-being was tied up with their mothers'. For example, the family support worker at St Thomas's High School, speaking of Kat's social worker, said: 'she knows that if Kat is okay, the mum is okay and vice versa, if the mum is okay, Kat is okay'.

Where the girls perceived their mothers to be vulnerable, or relationships affecting them to be fragile, there was an impact on their participation in school. Sometimes this impact took the form of non-attendance, while at other times it was apparent in challenging behaviour. There were signs that the case study girls' experience of school was affected by their strong alignment of their interests with those of their families, and particularly of their mothers. For most girls, where families are socially, emotionally and economically stable, the support is reciprocal. For the girls here, family responsibilities in some measure undermined the extent and the form of their participation in school. Although the ostensible reasons for girls' exclusions are the same as the reasons for boys, it may be that underlying factors are different. Indications from this small sample were that girls' exclusion linked more closely to relationships and responsibilities within the family. The small number of girls in this study means that further investigation of gendered causes of exclusions would be needed before conclusions could be drawn.

The boys in this study were negotiating diverse masculinities. Those differences were reflected in their attitudes towards family, and affected the impact their exclusions had on their families. Autonomy and self-determination were highly prized by a number of boys in this study. Sometimes this encompassed responsibility for family members and at other times it caused a separating out of boys' interests from their families. The transition from boyhood to manhood entailed boys claiming and being accorded increased power and status in the domestic domain (Mac an Ghaill, 1994). This was apparent in the case studies but boys' claims for increased power and status took very different forms. For some, it led to a separating out of their interests from their parent(s), most usually their mother; while for others, their negotiation of masculinity was pursued through their acceptance of responsibility for family and home. In the latter category was Dougie who lived with his mother and his younger sister. On a residential experience, during which Dougie's mother had been in hospital, Dougie had been very anxious about her, and repeatedly phoned the hospital. Dougie's concern for his mother extended to the research. Although she had given permission for Dougie and herself to be interviewed, Dougie did not want his mother to be interviewed. This was an interesting inversion of the protocols for gaining consent and it seemed to stem from his desire to save her from the pain of discussing difficult issues relating to Dougie's behaviour.

In contrast were boys who, unlike the case study girls, did not openly align their well-being with their mothers' and seemed to have moved beyond the influence of parents. Many of the excluded boys lived with their single mothers and, in two cases, those mothers had mental health problems. Craig and Andy's mother reported that Andy has been violent towards her, kicking, swearing and screaming when she tried to get him to attend a behaviour interview at the school with her. In Craig's file it was noted that his mother had no control over her sons, that she had her arm broken by Craig and had been kicked out of the house by them. Andy and Craig's mother was willing to come to school when required but the deputy headteacher (DHT) reported that she was ineffective in her efforts to influence her sons and the lack of home supervision had resulted in them having a great deal of autonomy in their lives. Speaking of Andy, one of his teachers said, 'I get the feeling that he is his own keeper or whatever. He is in charge of his own decisions and nobody else's. He really does not give a damn about theirs' (RE teacher).

Some boys were exercising a surprising measure of control unmediated by caring adults. Andy and Craig were just 12 years old but they were making decisions about how to live their lives. This autonomy did not assist their participation in schooling. They lacked the routines and regulation governing the lives of most 12-year-olds and were frequently absent from school.

Boys' 'under-achievement' has been attributed to the absence of positive role models at home and in primary school in particular with a negative impact on boys' engagement with schooling. Several professionals did feel that some of the boys in the study had seen masculinities being done in ways that were both influential and unhelpful to them in negotiating their own identities. Ross was cited as one such boy. Ross's attitude to his mother is protective but he sees her as exerting very little control over him. 'My older pals they will be like that "Your maw will ground you and all that". She tries, she does try and discipline me, but I am just not listening'.

Sometimes, case study boys indicated that they valued and relied upon professional support. Ross, for example, had developed a positive relationship with the home/school link worker and cared about the good opinion of this member of the school staff. Behaviour support teachers, too, sometimes had significant influence over pupils who were in difficulty. The agency demonstrated by boys could bring them into direct opposition to professional advice, for example, Andy and Craig both declined referrals to psychological services in spite of the urgings of the behaviour support teacher. In this study, where boys exercised considerable autonomy, overcoming their mothers' attempts to control their behaviour, there were signs that this was part of their negotiation of dominant masculinities. Alongside that, the home circumstances of these boys were fragile with boys' mothers receiving help from the Social Work Department and with the possibility that the boys would be transferred to residential school.

Poverty

In this study, seven case study pupils were registered for free school meals (FSM) and there were further indications coming through from interviews that a number of the case study pupils were living in poverty. Disparities exist between eligibility, registration and uptake of FSM (SEED, 2007) so it is possible that additional case study pupils were eligible but had opted not to register. This unwillingness has been attributed mainly to the stigma of being labelled as poor (Storey and Chamberlin, 2001; Granville et al. 2006). Poverty was seen to undermine pupils' participation in schooling and to deny them the benefits accruing from education, including formal credentials. This section will examine how economic circumstances impacted on case study pupils' experience of schooling through:

- a lack of material possessions;
- shame and embarrassment;
- stress on family relationships; and
- disruption to the regular routines helpful to participation in schooling.

Each of these is examined in turn as follows.

Lack of material resources exerted a pull away from school because some case study pupils had to earn money for themselves or to contribute to the family income. Some were working a significant (and illegal) number of hours. Pupils themselves cited their satisfaction that they earned income. One such pupil was Jack. In S3, he had already started to earn a living, working in a chip van two nights a week from 4.00–10.00 p.m. For these 12 hours he earned £30.00. Jack was the eldest of five children and his father had struggled to maintain the family in their own home after his wife's death. Jack indicated that when he was not at school, he helped his father with the shopping and with other household chores. Unlike many of the boys in this study, Jack was a loner and there were indications that his self-exclusion or withdrawal from the social networks related to poverty. The whole group of case study pupils had very low involvement in school activities such as sport, music or drama and school trips. Schools are often aware of the economic conditions of pupils' lives but, in offering a range of extra-curricular activities to pupils, are sometimes not aware of the costs entailed, for example, for transport.

Poverty had the effect of limiting participation in the social life of the school for some pupils but that did not mean that they were not part of very strong social networks, based in their own neighbourhoods. For some adolescents, those locally based networks were more attractive and more important than anything offered by the school, irrespective of costs. Schools attempt to build the social and cultural capitals of their pupils by offering a range of opportunities within and beyond the formal curriculum. Alternative forms of social capital are available to pupils, as are multiple opportunities to increase those capitals with the peer group and in local communities. While some pupils opt in to what is offered by the school, others, from the same community, turn away from school. What determines these choices? Poverty limits the range of options but the likelihood of disengagement may be increased as a result of experience of education itself. In any educational sphere, those who feel themselves to be less well regarded are more likely to disengage (Ingram, 2009).

For pupils living in poverty, their homes did not afford the social space that would enable them to have friends to stay or even to visit. The physical restrictions of home were a disincentive to using it for social purposes but also coming through was embarrassment about furnishings. The family support worker reported that Kat, one of the case study girls, was in this position: 'I think she feels embarrassed at the home situation, sort of furniture-wise, because it is very poor inside. I mean it is as clean as mum could possible keep it but, obviously, she is limited with the income'.

The limitations of home as a social space may have particular repercussions for girls who generally did not access public spaces as easily as boys, although there were signs in this study that girls used their friendships with boys to sponsor their social participation in outside spaces such as streets and parks. Few other social sites would have been open to young people because many such places levy charges.

Survival issues dominated the lives of case study pupils and their families. Pupils' participation in schooling was affected not only by material deprivation itself but also by the stresses arising from poverty caused by poor housing, alcohol and drug abuse, mental health problems and very limited opportunities for recreation. Most of the young people, and all of the girls, were closely aligned with their families and some of them took very practical responsibility for them, for example, by working part time, helping with housework or caring for a parent with mental health problems. One girl's family received support from the Social Work Department, mostly in relation to welfare rights and benefits but also to make sure that *mum was okay and that the family situation was settled* (family support worker). Stress and emotional insecurity loomed large in the lives of case study pupils, rendering some of them edgy and angry and shaping their engagement with schooling. Where the girls perceived their mothers to be vulnerable, or relationships affecting them to be fragile, there was an impact on their participation in school. Sometimes, this impact took the form of non-attendance while at other times it was apparent in challenging behaviour. Lorraine's fraught relationship with her mother contributed to her exclusion. Having been referred to the assistant headteacher (AHT) for not wearing full school uniform, Lorraine was angry that she was being treated unfairly since other pupils were also wearing incomplete uniforms. The AHT indicated his intention to involve Lorraine's mother at this point, causing Lorraine some anguish:

> Mr M was phoning my mum at work and my mum doesn't like people phoning her at work, like, about me . . .
> (Lorraine)

Lorraine's angry reaction – she swore at the AHT – led directly to her exclusion. In other cases a phone call to alert parents was the means of averting an exclusion. In Lorraine's case, the phone call threatened to further stess her relationship with her mother.

In addition, poverty affected family routines and made difficult the patterns required for regular participation. Although their families seemed to be endorsing their children's disengagement from schooling, the circumstances in which they were living their lives offered very little by way of choice. There were indications that boys, in particular, were moving beyond the influence of their parent(s), most usually mothers, especially where those parents were pre-occupied with survival issues. Ross' attendance in S1 had been poor. His record showed 129 absences from a possible 369 openings at time of interview, giving an attendance rate of 65.04 per cent. Only two of Ross' absences were unauthorised, indicating that his mother knew about, and had sanctioned, his frequent non-attendance. Ross reported in an interview, 'ma is dead soft, she gives in too easy'. Similarly, 12-year-old Craig lived with his mother who had mental health problems and who had great difficulty in helping her son to organise his life. Craig reported that when he or his brother was excluded, they were allowed to go out because their mother:

> doesn't like to keep us in. She likes us to go out and all and play football and stuff. She likes us to go out. She doesn't like keeping us in. She doesn't feel it is right if she keeps us in.
> (Craig)

The boys' mothers were reported as being very responsive to school contacts but their personal circumstances made it difficult for them to exercise control over their sons. Personal, social and material resources are needed to establish and maintain the routines required to ensure continuity of school experience, let alone to secure successful outcomes for one's children. Even where mothers were able to work hard to support their children's educational attainment, working-class women were disadvantaged in their efforts because, relative to middle-class women, they lacked both the resources and the social power to influence school practices (Reay, 1998: 163). For mothers living in poverty, the work needed to ensure successful outcomes from schooling took second place to issues of survival.

The main gender difference in exclusions is in the overall pattern where year after year boys predominate. Explanation for this was sought partly in considering if and how poverty impacted differently on boys and girls. There was some evidence that case study girls' poor attendance, though no worse than boys', might have been for different reasons in that they experienced more of a pull to be at home.

Aggression and violence

During the 1990s, violence in schools became a major concern. A number of exclusions of case study boys were for violent and aggressive behaviour. Only some of the case study pupils were violent – it is not suggested here that violence was a pervasive feature. This section will consider how these forms of behaviour are related to the negotiation of particular gender identities.

Understandings of what constitutes violent behaviour have expanded to include new categories such as being ostracised by the social group, name-calling and 'dirty looks'. The expansion of the definition of aggression has introduced a gender dimension since some forms of what is classified as violent behaviour have traditionally been associated with feminine behaviour. The aggressive behaviour which all three girls in this study manifested, was the result of one-off provocation, rather than symptomatic of a universal anger towards others. Their femininities encompassed aggressive behaviour, for example, sticking up for themselves and being prepared to defend family members. If aggression and violence are construed in this way, girls had a great deal in common with some boys in the study who valorised aggression and violence as a form of social competence. Brown (2005: 72) endorses this view in noting that social competence and agency of this nature is rarely, if ever, formally acknowledged in educational establishments such as schools, particularly in girls.

It is hard to see how schools could acknowledge aggression as a form of social competence when its manifestations from girls and boys were often associated with intimidation and bullying. A number of the boys who had been excluded exalted physical fitness and strength. Charlie was 14, tall, with an athletic build. He was very keen on sport and he had considerable ability as a boxer for which had won medals. In addition, he was good at athletics, swimming and played for a local football club. Not surprisingly, he liked physical education and felt he was doing well there. Charlie had been excluded five times during the previous session, amounting to 21 days of school missed. His first exclusion had come in P6, although he indicated that he had been in trouble since his early days in primary. His first exclusion in primary school was for fighting and subsequent exclusions had also been for aggressive behaviour mainly towards teachers, although he had also punched a pupil. His most recent exclusion had been as one of a group of 15 pupils who had gone to a nearby non-denominational school to seek a fight with pupils there. It was not clear if the motives for this gang confrontation had been sectarian or territorial.

In lessons, Charlie asserted himself in ways that were very challenging for the teacher and disruptive of the lesson. Charlie was observed in maths when he became very persistent with requests to go to the toilet, all of which were turned down by the teacher. Eventually, he was taken from the room by the principal teacher (PT) maths. During the time when Charlie was seeking to leave the room, other pupils incited him to some extent. A boy at the back shouted to him that he should just leave anyway while Kat started her own line of pressure to go to wash her hands. The maths teacher later described Charlie as having to have confrontation. This was backed up by Charlie's drama teacher who described him as very self-centred and physically aggressive. He had been unwilling to take instructions from the teacher and had been verbally aggressive towards him.

Charlie demonstrated the same aggressive qualities towards his fellow pupils, too. He worked mainly with boys and he was very domineering, even physically aggressive towards them. He wanted to be the centre of attention. In home economics, when he did speak to other pupils, he did so fairly aggressively: *What are you doing touching my . . . ?* The teacher – a young woman – used Charlie's board and ingredients to demonstrate techniques to others but, even before this, it was clear that other pupils paid attention to Charlie. He was influential; other pupils regularly came to see what he was doing but he paid little attention to anyone. Charlie was reported as unwilling to work with others unless he was in charge.

The aggression which pervaded Charlie's relationships in school may be interpreted in some contexts as a form of social competence but in school it would more likely be interpreted as bullying. There was some indication that other pupils might be scared of Charlie. He had a reputation as a fighter. One teacher reported that younger children, on seeing his jotter in her class, would comment and ask her about him. And while he might be exercising agency in his relationships with teachers, he was also capable of losing self-control. Indeed, some of the fear he inspired may well have been because of this volatility, as well as his physical capacities. Charlie acknowledged that he loses his temper in class but said this was usually because he has been blamed for things he has not done. Charlie's home economics teacher described him thus:

> If I say something that displeases him you see like a wee flicker that crosses his face and he starts to get angry. He can set off for any reason and it can be very, very small things . . . he doesn't tend to like being told what to do so at times he kind of comes up against me because he wants to do things his way and I try to get round him to more my way . . . He's got a very short fuse and that is what most people would say about him. A very, very short fuse.
>
> (Home economics teacher)

Charlie was negotiating a very dominant masculinity and aggression and violence as part of that process. There was agency in his use of physical prowess to attract status with his peer group. Wherever it occurs, this behaviour is very challenging. In schools, it is linked to the well-being of other pupils.

It is not argued here that aggression was a dimension of the class culture of the case study sample. It featured more fluently than that in the experience of pupils. Violence was not always valorised by the peer group. Some case study pupils with a history of violence were ostracised. For example, Alan had been excluded many times for a range of unacceptable behaviours. He *winds up* other people, annoying teachers and other pupils, he shouts out in class and has sometimes been violent towards other pupils. One-to-one he is described as 'very plausible', but he has caused real difficulties in and out of the classroom. Alan's aunt thinks he may have ADHD but the school thinks this is not the case. The DHT reported that the more serious of Alan's exclusion incidents took place outside the classroom and frequently involved bullying or harm to other people. For example, he had twice set fire to other pupils' hair while standing outside in the line waiting to go into the classroom. On the first occasion, no-one had actually seen him do this and it could not be proved but he did the same thing again. This time he was seen by many others who were reported as queueing up to 'grass' on him. The AHT indicated that Alan seemed to have no close friends among his peers. His aggression entirely distanced him from his peer group, causing him to be ostracised.

There was evidence that some aggression was not the result of agency, but of its opposite, frustration at a lack of control over one's own life. Jack was very angry about his family circumstances and this had repercussions for his behaviour in school. Commenting on Jack's behaviour, the DHT indicated that his big problem was his temper: 'He just cannot control his temper. He just flares up and is almost uncontrollable. On a one-to-one basis, he is great. I really like him and can hold a good conversation with him'.

Jack was very self-aware. When interviewed he conveyed that he knew that his temper caused problems and he knew that some of his teachers were frustrated because they could not teach him properly when his schooling was so discontinuous. Jack's aggression and violence brought him no status with his male peer group. It was the result of a loss of control and was interpreted as such by the school. Jack attended classes on anger management, a common strategy in behaviour support bases but one unlikely to be helpful for pupils who, unlike Jack, were using aggression consciously to negotiate particular kinds of masculinity.

Case study pupils were the victims as well as the perpetrators of violence, sometimes in the community and sometimes in their homes. School staff indicated that some case study pupils were known to have been physically abused at home and, in one case, to have witnessed the physical abuse of his mother by his father. Another boy, Eddie, was in S3 and had a long history of exclusions starting in primary school. Often in primary and in secondary schools his exclusions were for fighting, although there were other reasons as well, 'like sometimes it was carry on, sometimes it was fighting and then sometimes it was stealing and sometimes it was other stuff, like cheeky to teachers and that' (Eddie).

He was the youngest in a large family and his parents had been supportive of the school when Eddie has been excluded. However, by Eddie's account that support involves the threat of physical abuse, particularly from his mother, once he is back at home:

> . . . I am more scared of my Ma than my Da . . . because even though my ma's wee-er than me – she's wee-er than me and I am quite wee – I am more scared of my Ma than my Da. My Ma is a very vicious woman.
> (Eddie)

The DHT indicated that Eddie was a very likeable boy – 'blond and bubbly' – and that he would try to charm teachers. His exclusions had usually been short term but there had been a number of them, usually occurring when teachers could not take any more. The DHT reported that Eddie would cry when he got into trouble and she took this as a sign of his immaturity. However, Eddie himself reported that he feared going home after he had been excluded because of his mother's violent reactions.

Violence was a feature in the lives of many of the case study boys. Sometimes they were its victims but in certain cases violence and the threat of violence were used as part of the negotiation of masculinities in school settings.

Future lives

Across the four schools there was a high level of consistency in the occupational choices of pupils. The boys in the study almost all cited working-class jobs as their preferred future occupation. Although a number of the case study pupils were recognised as bright by their schools, only 1 of the 17 boys indicated his intention of proceeding to higher education. This was Ewen, the only middle-class pupil in the study, who did not specify a preference for a job but he did convey a sense of having choices and being in control of his future. 'Well, I want to get a good job and settle, well, I might not settle down too quickly . . . There is so much I want to do' (Ewen).

Given the wider circumstances of their lives, it is possible that the occupational choices the other boys were making were realistic constructions of their futures. Boys themselves saw traditional routes for working-class boys, including the armed services, as a desirable option. Eddie wanted to join the RAF when he left school. This had always been his ambition because his Uncle Tam had been in the RAF and had gained a great deal from it. Eddie cited three advantages of joining up:

> it's good pay, you get a lot of education from it and like if I need a house, because I have done honour for – don't know how to put it – because I have done honour for the – I can't get it out. . . . If I work well in there and I need a house, instead of waiting 17 years for another house, instead of waiting that long they put you up fast instead of waiting . . . because I have honoured Scotland and whatever.
>
> (Eddie)

Shortly after, Eddie remembered a further reason for joining the RAF:

> like there is another reason I have always wanted to go to the RAF because say if I have got a car I can take it in and I can get the mechanics and the engineers and all that to fix it for me, do it up.
>
> (Eddie)

The advantages cited by Eddie point to his valuing security of home and job and to the importance in his eyes of acquiring marketable skills. Similarly, Sam's mother indicated that he had shown some interest in joining the army and that, should he pursue this option, she would support him. 'The way I look at it is, they are in the army, they are disciplined, they are going to get a career. They have got everything they want in the services . . .'(Sam's mother).

As previously indicated a number of pupils were earning and the boys in particular spoke of the need to get a good job and cited this as a main reason for continuing in school. 'A good job' meant a trade. Many of the boys interviewed aspired to have a trade – car mechanic was mentioned by three of the boys as what they hoped for in the future. Andy wanted to be a plumber and said that he was prepared to stay on at school to help achieve this. Andy was exceptional in the group of boys because his academic performance had held up in spite of several periods of exclusion. He was in some Credit classes in S4 and was expected to do Highers in S5. For other boys, the pattern was a gradual falling away in attainment and engagement with schooling. There were fears for Ross who was in S1 and just 12 years old. The concern was that he would make wrong choices:

> Ross will probably be running a gang in Glasgow when he is twenty-one
> ... He is not at the stage yet when he needs to choose but soon, he is going
> to have to decide 'What way am I going to go?'
>
> (DHT)

For the school's part, the DHT felt that there were a small number of staff who would be prepared 'to go the extra mile' because Ross was very bright but that he was uncertain whether the school would be able to engage Ross, commenting, 'It is in the balance'. In primary school, because he was good at maths, Ross and his mother had thought that he would become a chartered accountant. Now, at 12 and because of his interest in motor bikes he thought he might become a car mechanic.

There were only three girls in this study and so it is not possible to detect patterns in their choices. One teacher commented that, in general, girls were more focused in school because their futures were clearer to them. They knew they were going to be a teacher or a nurse whereas for boys, many of the traditional options had been closed off for them. This view was justified in relation to one of the case study girls, Gill who indicated that she intended to stay on until S6 and then she planned on going to College. She wanted to become a midwife. She was aware that she would first need a nursing qualification before going on to specialise. She seemed very focused and very clear about how to reach her goal. It was interesting that her teachers were quite unaware of these ambitions. They believed that, in spite of Gill being bright, she would not stay on after 'S' Grades. All three girls were acknowledged to have a range of abilities but their schools did not predict career paths for them, even for Gill who had her own career path mapped out.

There was little practical institutional support for boys either in moving towards their preferred occupations, although all four schools offered a great deal of personal support to pupils in difficulty. Teachers saw boys' aims towards jobs as car mechanics or scafffolders as a result of pupils' limited horizons and believed schools had a part to play in raising the aspirations of boys:

> I keep saying to C—, 'Why don't you just get your head down, pick something you would really, really, love to do' and he can't see why a scaffolder isn't the best thing he can ever do. And obviously, education has a part to play in that.
>
> (PT)

The boys themselves generally saw school as instrumental in helping them to get the kinds of jobs they hoped for but they had very vague notions of what was needed by way of qualifications. Several cited contacts among friends and family as the means by which they would get a job. School, then, served very unclear purposes for the boys in the study, exerting over them an arbitrary authority but offering limited practical help in their preparations for the future.

Sometimes, the reality of their predicament was beginning to become clear to some of the boys who had been excluded. Joe hoped to be a joiner but he recognised that it would be difficult for him to get the qualifications because he was no longer allowed into the Technical Department. Similarly, Charlie had hoped to be a physical education teacher or a boxer when he was older. He recognised that he would need Highers to pursue his ambition to be a teacher but he did not think things at school were settled enough for this to be realistic. In fact, staff had expressed doubts that Charlie would finish his schooling in St Thomas's – such was the level of disruption he caused. For other boys, too, there was some pessimism. The DHT was fearful for the future of two of the case study boys as there was a strong possibility that they would be taken into the care of the local authority. Placement in a residential school would perhaps be the most likely outcome for them. Such a placement would not necessarily be a bad thing for the boys but the school certainly saw such a decision as, at least in part, indicative of the school's failure.

Commentators have noted that the social and economic changes of the past 20 or 30 years have led to a heightened sense of risk and a greater individualisation of experience among young people (Furlong and Cartmel, 1997; Giddens, 1990). Insecurity now marks all transitions from childhood to adulthood. Ross articulated his own sense of insecurity about the future:

> I know for me I don't think. I just take life as it comes . . . you don't know if you are going to be here in four year's time so why not just live for the moment? Because you don't know if your family . . . and you don't know if you are going to be there.
>
> (Ross, S1)

In facing uncertain futures and highly individualised choices, the boys in this study differed from Willis' 'lads' whose futures in industrial capitalism were all too evident to them and who moved towards those futures as a group. The individualisation of experience of transition from school to adult life contrasted with the strong collective identities valued by both boys and girls, for example, in their strong sense of community and locality, and in their support of football teams (Nayak, 2003). Education can open up options for pupils but the real circumstances of their lives may motivate against pursuing those options. For example, considerable financial resources are required for participation in higher education, resources not available to most of the families in this study. There was a sense in which the pupils in this study were moving into adult life more quickly than their middle-class counterparts who would expect their transitions into adulthood to be more extended, scaffolded for them by their families through, for example, continued financial support.

There were echoes of Willis' *Learning to Labour* in the ways working-class boys in this study constructed their futures from their experience of the lives of those around them. Case study pupils were moving towards independence, speaking of joining the army or becoming a car mechanic, jobs which, for some of them, marked a lowering of expectations as adult life approached. Family and community could be seen as limiting the aspirations of girls and boys – a view articulated by teachers. Alternatively, the paths pupils were trying to map out for themselves could be the only paths open to them, offering them financial independence in their teens and security into the future. Willis' analysis has been criticised as attributing no individual agency to the 'lads'. The same economic determinism operated on the future lives of most of the pupils in this study in spite of the recognised quality of the secondary schools they attended.

Analyses of social exclusion have argued that gender and class inequalities are unchanged and continue to ensure the reproduction of advantage and disadvantage among the younger generation. The Organisation for Economic Co-operation and Development (OECD) report emphasises the importance of school as *the key institutional point at which the transmission of disadvantage has the most chance of being broken* (Teese et al. 2007: 110). Questions are opened up, then, as to the role schooling should play in the lives of young people living in poverty. There were signs that case study pupils were moving away from schooling as they reached adolescence; their formal exclusions were part of a wider pattern of disengagement from schooling (Lloyd, 2005). The challenge for Scottish schools, according to Teese et al. (2007: 60) is how to maintain its overall high level of performance *while substantially improving the capacity of poorer children to benefit from school*. The political challenge is clear: the abolition of child poverty is likely to extend the benefits of schooling to a wider group. In the meantime, the educational challenge remains.

Initiatives arising from *Better Behaviour – Better Learning* (SEED, 2000a) have had a positive impact. As noted in other studies (Boyd, 2007; Stead et al. 2007), home/school link workers, in particular, had gained the trust and confidence of some of the case study pupils who were experiencing greatest difficulty in their home lives and whose parents may have been further alienated from school as a result of their child's exclusion (Parsons, 1999; Hanafin and Lynch, 2002; McDonald and Thomas, 2003). As a result of the support they received, young people were perhaps less angry and brittle in school settings, more able to deal with the stresses of their lives, and had access to an adult who could mediate on their behalf with the school. While this helped maintain pupils' connection to schooling, and reduced exclusions, it did not assist with their participation in the curriculum. The flexibility offered by systems of behaviour support has been helpful for schools (Munn et al. 2000; Head et al. 2003; Kane et al. 2004) but it has also increased their capacity for curricular exclusion. More flexible ways of organising the curriculum could help pupils to make the most of positive connections some pupils had with some teachers. A core plus options curricular structure, separated out from age and stage correspondences, would enable all pupils to spend more time in areas where they were doing well and where their motivations were higher. According greater scope to pupils and families generally in planning their curriculum, within more diverse curriculum pathways, would be consistent with increasing participation in schooling more generally. Dyson *et al.* (2003), having reviewed the literature on school inclusion, identified the need for schools to build close relations with parents and communities based on developing a shared commitment to inclusive values.

Conclusion

Most of the case study pupils experienced some measure of social exclusion in their lives. Poverty was seen to undermine pupils' and families' engagement with schooling and exclusion from school exacerbated that effect. For some of the case study pupils and especially for girls, family exerted a pull away from school because of their concerns with the well-being of their mothers. Case study boys sought to negotiate a range of maculinities, ensuring varied attitudes towards family, sometimes very strained relationships, and different effects caused by their exclusion. Where exclusions were experienced as a punishment, this was because of the impact on families. It was difficult to detect exclusions serving any purpose other than punishment for the case study pupils and their families. Exclusions caused extra pressure within some very fragile family relationships. In addition, the alienating effect of exclusions on families' attitudes to schooling lasted beyond the period of the exclusion, with parents' voicing their anxiety about routine contacts with schools. This negative and ongoing effect of exclusion seemed to be unrecognised by schools. Parents' failure to participate was attributed to their lack of interest in their children's school progress. Relationships with schooling were precarious for many of the working-class families in this study.

Pupils' futures also were uncertain and boys, in particular, conveyed this sense of insecurity. Schools were seen as helpful in enabling boys to make the transition to their adult lives but only in a general way. The scaffolding they needed, and which is provided by middle-class families, was not there for them. Some of this is economic – their families lacked the financial means to support them through prolonged education and boys themselves wished to earn money – but the reasons were also cultural. Boys cited jobs they knew about from their own direct experience. These issues and others arising from the two previous chapters will be discussed in the next chapter.

Chapter 7

Improving participation in schooling

> Sometimes they are a bit of an enigma to me... I would say that all of them are probably bright enough to play their future out so differently, but they just can't.
> (Behaviour support teacher)

The previous three chapters have outlined findings with regard to the identities of excluded pupils, the school processes shaping those identities and the broader circumstances of pupils' lives affecting their engagement with schooling. This chapter will summarise those findings to address how exclusion from school related to girls' and boys' negotiation of gender and social class identities in school and beyond school. Then themes of masculinities, femininities and social class will be discussed in greater depth. Implications for policy and for the development of schooling will be considered in the final section.

Summary

Social class was a permeating feature of pupils' cultural identities. This was particularly apparent in the 'Ned' affiliations of most of the girls and boys. That aspect of their identity was highly embodied in dress and physical appearance and, in addition, several boys during their interviews proudly proclaimed themselves to be Neds. That affiliation has been anathematised in media accounts and is associated with criminal and anti-social behaviour. In asserting that they were Neds, the boys were re-appropriating the term and attempting to valorise the value system of Neds, for example, in a commitment to loyalty to friends above all else. They were also consciously associating themselves with the socially marginalised as a matter of pride. They embraced Ned identity as a cultural expression of their social exclusion. Similarly, their strong sense of belonging to a particular locality conveyed that social exclusion was not a source of stigma for them. For the most part those localities were very unattractive environments, such as the 1960s housing schemes, but the boys had strong affiliations to their communities. These local affiliations enabled a collective identity – something the boys and girls enjoyed and pursued through their territorial battles with neighbouring localities.

Sectarianism around Catholic and Protestant identities cuts across social classes in Scotland and is associated particularly with support for Glasgow Celtic and Glasgow Rangers Football Clubs, and to a lesser extent, with other football clubs. The Scottish Government has established anti-sectarian legislation and, through a number of initiatives, is attempting to defeat sectarian behaviour. For some young people sectarian identities were tied up, not just with religious identities and football support, but also with belonging to particular places and with originating from long-established working-class communities. Sectarianism therefore entailed layers of identity not easily changed.

Gender identities were found to be complex with boys and girls playing out gender through allegiances as well as oppositions. Girls were seen to benefit from those allegiances; there was evidence that friendships with boys enabled girls to negotiate less conventional or 'tomboy' femininities, to 'act out' in ways very similar to boys, for example, by joining in gang fights. In discussing feminine identities, the term 'ladette' was not used by any of the participants but girls were noted as moving fluidly between 'tomboy' and 'glamour' identities, depending upon the social circumstances.

Where girls could negotiate a range of femininities, some boys were impelled towards the negotiation of a particular and dominant form of masculinity. These negotiations demanded the demonstration of physical strength and aggression, especially when used to defend or advance the interests of the peer group and the community. High status within the peer group was the reward for the successful negotiation of particular kinds of masculinities but many boys found the pursuit of that kind of identity difficult and even dangerous sometimes because of its associations with violence. Some boys were trying to negotiate these masculinities in school. These negotiations brought them into conflict with teachers, occasionally at the deliberate instigation of the boys themselves and resulting in their exclusion. Exclusions were shown as a link to the negotiation of masculine identities, particularly hegemonic masculinities, in ways that did not generally apply to the negotiation of feminine identities. Girls who were excluded were far fewer in number but they were excluded for the same reasons as boys, and had affiliations to the same social and cultural groups.

Schools as well as pupils were shown to be actively involved in the negotiation of pupil identities. Schools limited the range of identities open to pupils, for example, in their assessment of abilities, and through the classifying of pupils according to ability. Some exclusions were seen to arise from pupils' attempts to resist schools' labelling of them. A 'learning difficulties' label was particularly unwelcome and, in preference, boys were seen to create a 'challenging behaviour' label for themselves. Behaviour and learning were sometimes in tension, with very able pupils consigned to low-ability sets because of their challenging behaviour. Sometimes, schools were able to use a positive attribution of ability to encourage boys' to abandon, even temporarily in a particular curricular area, their oppositional attitudes. Boys making these accommodations were secretive about them wishing not to compromise their status with their peer group. For schools, behaviour was always the dominant factor. Organisation of the curriculum was such that pupils whose behaviour was challenging in some areas could not participate in other curriculum areas, even though their motivation and their ability there were acknowledged as very high.

Transition from primary to secondary school marked a significant change in some pupils' relationship with schooling. Pupils who had never been excluded in primary school experienced great difficulty in secondary and sometimes multiple exclusions in first and second year. The array of relationships, expectations and negotiations required by the complex organisation of secondary schools caused them to falter. A few of the boys in this position were seen to adopt very challenging behaviour which they conveyed as an attempt to negotiate hegemonic masculinity, even though there were no signs that their peer group accorded them this status. Not all case study pupils experienced secondary school so negatively. Some pupils about whom there was great concern preferred the breadth and the diversity of the secondary-school experience. They had accumulated bad behaviour records in primary school and communicated that secondary school had brought a welcome fresh start. Some of those pupils had very good relationships with one or more members of staff. During the interviews, these positive points of contact came across as being highly valued by the pupils concerned.

Family shaped children's engagement with schooling. Gender differences were detected in case study girls' and boys' alignments with their families, affecting their participation in schooling. The case study girls were close to their mothers and saw their interests as merged with their mothers', whereas case study boys were more likely to have distanced themselves from their parents', often their mother's, influence and control. Sometimes their autonomy was used benevolently and protectively towards their mothers and younger siblings but boys were more likely than girls to convey their independence from family influence. Alignment with family and separation from it could be equally unhelpful in shaping girls' and boys' engagement with schooling. Boys who exercised a great deal of personal autonomy were too young to use this well and were greatly at risk. Girls whose mothers were in very difficult personal circumstances were themselves affected by those circumstances, the resulting stress exacerbating the possibility of their exclusion. Although the reasons for girls' and boys' exclusions were the same, the underlying pressures on boys and girls leading to their exclusion, may be different. There were too few girls in this study to pursue this possible gender difference.

Family involvement in exclusions was mediated by social class. Exclusions were an effective punishment, that is, a deterrent for some pupils but only if their parents backed the school's action and maintained the punitive effect at home. Where parents were unable to sustain that position, exclusion served neither as a punishment nor as a deterrent. Parents' capacity to support actively the school's action depended upon their economic and emotional resources. Some case study boys reported that their mothers did not wish them to be in the house during the period of their exclusion. For those families, exclusion served only to put further pressure on already fragile family relationships. Worse than that, there was evidence that pupils' exclusion impacted on families' longer-term engagement with school, further alienating them from an important mainstream service. Social class differences in exclusion were seen most clearly in the events leading to exclusion. There was evidence that where parents responded quickly to school concerns, the exclusion could be averted. Many of the parents in this study were unable to respond in this way, indeed some were not contactable by phone in the first place. Even when contact could be established, they were ill-equipped to act as the school would wish, for example, several mothers had mental health problems and needed a great deal of support to leave the house even for routine reasons.

Social class and gender were main themes in this study and in its findings. These broad social categories are not equally represented in the literature. Policy has not paid much attention to social class in school education. Gender and class are initially separated out in the discussion here but attempts are made to show how these aspects cut across each other in the identities of excluded pupils. The discussion here will conclude by considering the policy implications of the findings of the study.

Gender identities

Gender was identified by professionals and pupils alike as a factor in challenging behaviour. In considering gender here, masculinities will be considered first, followed by femininities and then the two will be considered together.

Masculinities

Interesting analyses were offered as to why so many more boys than girls were excluded. Of these, coming through most strongly was the notion of the culture of the peer group and its influence on boys' behaviour. Senior managers in schools as well as pupils themselves spoke of the pressure on boys to conform to that culture and explained that, when it was resistant to school as it often seemed to be, boys as a group showed up badly in the formal indicators of school success. There was evidence that the positioning of boys to schooling was linked to their pursuit of powerful and high-status masculinities (Mac an Ghaill, 1994; Epstein, 1997; Skelton, 1997; Jackson, 2002). Among the group of 17 case study boys were some who had been very successful in those negotiations and whose observed classroom behaviour was about the assertion of those masculinities to the undermining of teachers' authority and to the detriment of good classroom order. There were also other boys who had been less successful in negotiating hegemonic masculinity but who, nevertheless, sacrificed their relationships with teachers in order to pursue that aim. The study provided further evidence that the pursuit of *the impossible fiction of hegemonic masculinity* (Renold, 2004: 250) was difficult both for boys who were succeeding and for boys who were failing to establish this form of identity. Some boys were seen to juggle their claims to dominant, anti-school masculinities with their desire to use school to gain qualifications; other boys inhabiting the same kind of masculinity and from within the same peer group were moving rapidly away from school and towards less certain futures. Different choices here seemed partly to do with families and their capacity to provide stability and support for a lengthier adolescence in which sons would not be earning. In facing uncertain futures and highly individualised choices, the boys in this study differed from Willis' 'lads' whose futures were all too evident to them and who moved towards those futures as a group. The individualisation of experience of transition from school to adult life contrasted with the strong collective identities valued by both boys and girls, for example, in their sense of community and locality, and in their support of football teams.

Femininities

There were far fewer girls who were excluded and they were excluded less often than most of the boys. Tinklin (2003) identified a range of differences in girls' and boys' engagement with schooling, evident in attitudes towards schooling, experiences of peer culture, experiences of teaching and learning processes, curriculum content, assessment processes, teacher–pupil interactions, parental attitudes and in post-school opportunities. Most of these gender differences were not apparent in this study because its focus was on girls and boys who were excluded and had a good deal in common. The reasons for girls' exclusion were the same as the reasons why boys were excluded, that is, for general and persistent disobedience and for verbal abuse of teachers. Among the whole group of excluded pupils, there was some evidence that gender dichotomies broke down. Girls and boys valorised 'acting out' behaviour from both girls and boys and united with each other in school and out of school in locating the 'Other' in, for example, teachers, well-behaved pupils, young people from localities other than their own. This finding is at odds with some of the literature which has tended to characterise 'problem' girls as 'acting in' and as experiencing little commonality with boys (Brown and Gilligan, 1992; Osler *et al.* 2002). Further, adolescent girls were noted as experiencing a loss of voice or agency at that stage in their lives (McLaughlin, 2005). Agency will be discussed more fully further on but the girls in this study did not conform to this description. There were only three case study girls but there is evidence from beyond the study that the problem behaviour of girls was becoming more like the problem behaviour of boys. Media accounts have latched on to signs of growing 'ladette' behaviour with reports that the number of girls involved in crime in Scotland has increased by 40 per cent in five years (*The Herald* 18/9/2006). Similarly, recent statistics on school exclusions in Scotland (Scottish Executive, 2007) show a tenfold increase in the number of girls excluded from primary schools in the 2005/06 session. The number is still a small proportion of the total number of pupils excluded but there are indications that girls' behaviour is changing. This is not to say that girls are becoming more masculine but the range of femininities may be changing. This would be worth investigating further.

Gender oppositions and alignments

For boys and girls, there was strong evidence of the pull of the peer group and those peer groups were mixed-gender. In interviews, many pupils talked of their pleasure in their friends' company and of friendship as a mainspring in their lives. Friendship groups were locally as well as school based and were strongly rooted in particular communities and neighbourhoods. Sometimes, unacceptable behaviour in school was a demonstration of solidarity among the friendship group. But sometimes exclusions occurred because of non-school issues in friendship groups. The sense of belonging to a particular neighbourhood was bonding for young people and allowed girls and boys to transcend gender oppositions.

Girls' alignment of their interests with boys and in opposition to others in school could be viewed as a way of rejecting other, more passive, feminine identities. Through their friendships with boys, girls gained access to public spaces and to accepted norms of behaviour which might have been hard to reach in the company of other girls alone. Although these alignments offered advantages to girls, girls and boys were not eroding gender differences within them. Girls were able to alternate between 'tomboy' and 'glamour' images, to emphasise their differences from boys as well as their commonalities with boys. Similarly, Francis (2005:14), in her study of gender identity negotiations in classrooms, indicated that girls and boys cooperated to construct genders as opposite. The evidence in this study was that gender oppositions existed within broader gender alignments. Underpinning those alignments was a shared social class positioning. Girls and boys did not have equal power and status within these alignments. For example, although girls' aggressive behaviour was sometimes admired by boys, it was also spoken of in patronising ways. This would not necessarily be offensive to the girls in question. There was no sense of girls competing with boys for power and status within the peer group. In their aggressive behaviours and in their affiliations with boys, girls were not becoming more masculine, they were not trying to negotiate a high-status gender identity nor did they seem to be challenging boys' dominance. Rather, they were seeking to do femininities in fluid ways. Findings in this respect challenge newspaper reports claiming that an apparent deterioration in girls' behaviour means that girls are becoming more masculine (*The Herald*, 18/9/2006). Although it was harder for boys than for girls in this study to negotiate and occupy different kinds of gender identities, masculine identity was higher status than any kind of feminine identity (Reay, 2001: 164).

The distribution of power within gender relationships in this study shows no change since the 1980s when Willis' 'lads' dominated the girls of their acquaintance. What was different in this study was cross-gender friendships and affiliations, signalling a change since Willis' *Learning to Labour* and one that seems to impact upon the behaviours of girls, in particular. Most girls and boys in this study experienced social exclusion in addition to their exclusion from school. In a context which marginalises and sometimes vilifies their communities, it is perhaps not surprising that girls and boys pull together in order to differentiate themselves from other social groups. The next section will focus on social class as a dimension of the boys' and girls' identities affecting their exclusion from school.

Class identities

Social class has pervaded the findings of this study; its presence was apparent in case study pupils' articulation of Ned identities; in their experience of friendship, family and poverty; and in their constructions of their futures. Twenty-five years ago, Furlong (1985) noted that social class, educational attainment and challenging behaviour had long been linked but never acted upon:

> One of the most consistent findings to emerge from sociological research on indiscipline at school is that as a phenomenon it is far more common among working-class than among middle-class children . . . Pupils are seen as rejecting school because they are in the bottom stream or band, not because they are working-class. The fact that the majority of pupils in these bottom streams are working-class has remained a recognized but unexplored side issue.
>
> (Furlong, 1985: 152)

Decades ago, local comprehensive schools had been seen as a means of addressing schools' role in the distribution of social advantage and disadvantage (Willis, 1978; Ball, 1981; Reay, 1998). Ball (1981) investigated how social class emerged as a major discriminating factor in the distribution of success and failure in Beachside and charted the processes through which this occurred. His fieldwork, conducted in 1976, came early in the introduction of comprehensive schools in England and addressed the relationship between school stratification of pupils and the reproduction of wider social class structures. At the time of Ball's study, aspirations were that the new comprehensive system per se would bring about changes in the social class inequalities in education that had been caused by middle-class domination of the grammar schools (Ball, 1981: 31). Where in-school stratification continued through classes banded on ability, Ball's conclusion was:

> it is apparent that, while going some way towards solving the gross social problems and social inequalities which were a characteristic of the bipartite system, the streamed comprehensive school does produce an unstable, polarized social structure among its pupils, which in turn gives rise to considerable teaching and social control problems for teachers.
> (Ball, 1981: 283)

In this study, all four case study schools were local comprehensives. Although some placing requests were received and accepted, the schools generally reflected the social composition of the communities they served. Mixed-ability classes operated in S1 and S2 and streaming started in S3 as pupils prepared for Standard Grade certification. Most case study pupils did not fare well in in-school processes of selection. Even where abilities had been recognised at earlier stages of schooling, their attitudes and behaviour resulted in their allocation to lower sets. In one case, a case study boy was able to participate in a higher, more academic set by concealing his engagement with academic work (Jackson, 2002). Why do working-class children experience higher levels of disengagement and disaffection in school? This section will discuss the link between working-class identities and school exclusions, first by considering economic factors and then by exploring the class cultural identities of excluded pupils.

Pupils' economic background as a cause of exclusion

Throughout this study, professionals constructed the causes of exclusions as the social, economic circumstances within which young people lived their lives. Across the two phases of the research, professionals and pupils came from schools serving very different kinds of communities, from those showing some of the highest indicators of poverty in Scotland to very affluent, middle-class areas. None of those interviewed attributed levels of school exclusion to in-school causes and they varied in how far they thought in-school support systems could help. Where reductions in exclusions had been achieved, there was a view that only the 'soft edges' of exclusions had been tackled. What remained, it appeared, were much more hard-core difficulties beyond the school's influence. All of these professional respondents believed that exclusions would continue to be a necessary tactic for schools if they were to protect the educational experience of the majority. This deterministic view is very challenging for those concerned with social justice in school settings.

Many young people in the case study phase were preoccupied with survival issues. Their families were struggling with problems arising from poverty – poor physical and mental health, drug and alcohol addiction, inadequate housing and limited opportunities for social life and recreational activities. Most of the young people, and all of the girls, were closely aligned with their families and some of them took very practical responsibility for them, for example, by working part time, helping with housework or caring for a parent with mental health problems. Stress and emotional insecurity loomed large in the lives of case study pupils, rendering some of them edgy and angry and shaping their engagement with schooling. There was evidence that the negative effect of exclusions was felt through the additional stress placed on family relationships. Many pupils cited this as the main source of concern when they were excluded. A number of commentators have discussed the impact of poverty on the lives of children and particularly on their experience of school (Reay, 1998; Ridge, 2005). Its exclusionary effect on young people has been identified; the economic restrictions of some pupils' lives preventing full participation. Poverty has been noted as a factor in withdrawal or self-exclusion from school, forms of exclusion particularly affecting girls. This study provided evidence that the stresses of poverty contributed to formal exclusion from school.

Poverty also impacted on the procedures resulting in exclusion. Vincent (2000) argued that the reforms of the 1980s and the 1990s which claimed to increase parents' role in education had failed to recognise the differential positioning of parents to schooling, positions largely determined by social class. Some parents had little effect in the school processes which helped to shape their children's identity; other parents had a formative effect on schools' views of their children (Reay and Willian, 1999; Hamilton, 2002). Families' differential relationships to schooling were illustrated with regard to exclusion. Some parents could be proactive in allaying schools' concerns and forestalling the exclusion of their child. Other parents lacked the economic resources which would have enhanced their participation in their children's schooling, for example, they had no phone land lines and sometimes no contact phone at all. Once the exclusion had been effected, parents with greater resources were more likely to ensure the deterrent effect of the exclusion and prevent future exclusions. There was evidence, too, that young people living in poverty were more likely to experience the 'sending home' mechanism as exclusion. Their parents would sometimes find it harder to visit schools immediately and pupils were not re-admitted until parents had returned with them to school. Thus, pupils from working-class families, especially those living in poverty, were more likely to be excluded initially and more likely to be excluded on repeated occasions. For parents of those pupils, exclusion was experienced as a direct punishment for themselves and an experience which impacted on their engagement with schooling into the future (Parsons, 1999; Hanafin and Lynch, 2002; MacDonald and Thomas, 2003). Economic circumstances and their impact on families were a clear contributory factor to pupils' exclusion from school, and in their wider non-participation in education. Poverty and its associated problems had overwhelmed some of the families in this study and rendered them less able to intervene to forestall exclusion or to ensure its deterrent effect in the future.

In discussing their futures, the economic circumstances of young people's lives came to the fore. A number of them were earning and the boys in particular spoke of the need to get a good job and cited this as a main reason for continuing in school. Only 1 of the 20 case study pupils, the middle-class boy, indicated his intention of proceeding to higher education, although a number of the case study pupils were acknowledged as bright by their schools. Teachers saw this as a result of pupils' limited horizons and saw schools as having a part to play in raising the aspirations of boys.

Education can open up options for pupils but the collapse of the youth labour market does not allow many of those options to be followed through. In addition, the real circumstances of pupils' lives motivates against continuing in education. Case study pupils were moving towards independence, speaking of joining the army or becoming a car mechanic, jobs which for some of them marked a lowering of expectations as adult life approached.

In 2007, with 16.2 per cent of its children living below the poverty line, Britain was placed at the bottom of a children's well-being league table of advantaged nations (UNICEF, 2007). The argument here has been that poverty is one of the causes of school exclusion because of the stresses caused to pupils and families by material deprivation. Policy constructs the relationship between school exclusion and social exclusion as a causal one: school exclusions are seen to undermine pupils' education and to damage their prospects of gaining the skills and the credentials needed to gain more than low-skill jobs. The causal relationship between school- and social exclusion is two-way, however. Poverty also causes school exclusion but this side of the relationship is less conspicuous in policy. Families living in poverty are disadvantaged in their engagements with schooling: higher rates of exclusion are symptomatic of that disadvantage.

Class cultural identities and schooling

The working-class identities of young people in this study would not be shaped by relationships to the means of production. The old world of work was not open to the case study pupils and the values and forms of social organisation arising from work no longer prevailed for them. Three of the four case study schools in this study were in urban, post-industrial communities formerly dominated by the steel and mining industries. Aspects of traditional masculine working-class identities were evident among boys in this study, for example, they placed a high value on humour and the ability to entertain, solidarity with the peer group and a sense of belonging, the importance of sporting prowess, physical strength and fitness. Also very evident was young peoples' sense of being socially as well as physically anchored in working-class communities. Archer and Yamashita (2003: 119) noted that boys in their study in the north-east of England articulated a sense of belonging to a place as constituting an important part of their identities. This linked to their need to feel safe, to be known and accepted. This was true in this study but there was evidence that sense of belonging to one place was constructed also as not belonging to other places. Territorial conflicts figured largely in the lives of girls and boys interviewed.

It is hard to separate locality from community in the sense of belonging articulated by case study pupils. Belonging to a place could also be a metaphor for cultural affiliation. This class cultural identity came across in a number of ways but most conspicuously in their speech. It has not been possible in this thesis to convey the vibrancy of the dialect/language used by the pupils interviewed for this study but their speech was a confident assertion of their working-class, west-of-Scotland identities. Archer and Yamashita (2003: 119) detected agency in the ways in which working-class boys in their study in the north-east of England constructed their identities through speech, dress and physical presentation. They argued that the adoption of particular kinds of embodied masculinities would be likely to hinder the social mobility of the boys, for example, through job interviews. There was no indication from the young people in this study that they sought social mobility. Where pupils belong to socially excluded communities their strong and self-conscious sense of belonging may operate against educational achievement. The economic barriers to higher education were discussed earlier but it is possible that cultural factors also posed a barrier to participation in education beyond the compulsory phase of schooling. The credentials offered by educational success may have been viewed as threatening dislocation and cultural disconnection. It was noticeable that only the middle-class boy in this study saw a future for himself in higher education.

Working-class boys in this study constructed their futures from their experience of the working lives of those around them. Family and community could be seen as limiting the aspirations of girls and boys. School staff certainly articulated their role as countering those limited aspirations. Alternatively, the paths pupils were trying to map out for themselves could be the only paths open to them. Boys themselves, sometimes as young as 12 or 13, spoke of using the social connections available to them, intending to learn trades from uncles or family friends. The changes of the past 20 or 30 years have transformed youth transitions; these are now more individualised, extended and laden with risk (Furlong and Cartmel, 1997; Giddens, 1990). Awareness of risk came through, for example, in 12-year-old Ross' claims not to think about the future because it was too uncertain. Even before facing the prospect of adult life, many young people in this study lived in precarious circumstances; their security and the well-being of their families undermined by the stresses of poverty. But awareness of present circumstances and uncertain futures was shared and contributed towards a collective identity. Although young people perceived themselves as having to negotiate risk and insecurity at an individual level, they placed a high value on those collective identities. In contrast, Ball (2006) notes that the planning of an educational career by middle-class parents for their children *is denoted by particular kinds of planning and thoughtfulness* and that the middle classes are especially suited to this work (Ball, 2006: 266). Worry about risk, and the capacity to mediate it on behalf of children and young people, differentiates middle-class families from the families in this study. In the midst of social change, class inequalities remained constant (Gormley, 2003; Furlong and Cartmel, 2007).

Questions are opened up as to the role schooling should play in the lives of young working-class people. There were signs that case study pupils were moving away from schooling as they reached adolescence; their formal exclusions were part of a wider pattern of disengagement from schooling. In marked contrast to the principal teacher (PT) behaviour support suggestion that schools should raise pupils' aspirations, some schools have tried to increase engagement and counter disaffection by providing a more 'relevant' curriculum of basic skills and vocational courses. By attempting to engage pupils in this way, schools could be seen as preparing their pupils for lives of social exclusion. The development of school provision is discussed further on under the implications of the study.

The complexity of the identities pursued by young people in this study points to how important out-of-school influences were for adolescents. Archer and Yamashita (2003: 129) argue that education policy has taken too narrow a perspective on boys' relatively low attainment by attributing this to 'laddishness' and neglecting the impact of social and cultural change on the identities of working-class men. Gormley (2003) summarises these thus:

> Young people's relationships with family and friends have changed, their experiences of education and the labour markets have altered dramatically, while their leisure and lifestyle choices have developed in ways that reflect the post-industrial consumer culture that they are immersed in.

The experience of case study pupils reflected these changes. Implications for policy and schooling are discussed further on but first the question of agency in pupils' exclusion will be considered.

Agency and exclusions

Were pupils exercising agency in the processes leading to their exclusion? There were indications that oppositional attitudes to schooling were a matter of choice for some young people. For example, pupils such as Ross were seen to challenge teachers in classrooms in a deliberate and controlled way. On the other hand, there was evidence that factors such as poverty and pupils' views of their own futures impelled them towards conflict with schooling. Agency was detected in pupils' behaviour but not always in opposition to school.

The economic and social circumstances of some case study pupils' lives made engagement with schooling difficult and so their attendance could be seen as a considerable personal commitment in overcoming barriers to their participation. This section will consider directly how far and in what ways pupils were excluded as a result of their agency, or the agency of others.

Schooling became less and less important in the lives of some young people as they started secondary school and moved towards the school-leaving age at 16. Attendance declined and participation in voluntary school activities, for example, sports, was minimal for the group of excluded pupils. In many cases, this was in contrast to their engagement with primary education where some, but not all, excluded pupils had been happy, settled and engaged. Pupils could be seen as exercising choice in turning away from school as they grew up. The challenge they presented to school systems and to prevalent norms of behaviour could be interpreted as a means for adolescents to distance themselves from schooling. Their oppositional behaviour could be viewed as part of a conscious process of negotiating independent adult identities. Such a construction would not explain why the majority of excluded pupils are working-class adolescents.

Munn and Lloyd (2005) argue that agency in relation to excluded pupils opens up questions of responsibility, resistance and compliance both at individual and institutional levels (2005: 208). They argue that the concept is helpful in determining the extent to which the school has been the agent of exclusion, through, for example, the unfair behaviour of the teacher. Pupils in this study on occasions saw teachers as the cause of their exclusion, explaining their own anger and verbal abuse as having been provoked by teachers' failure to treat them with respect. There were also some indications that pupils believed their exclusion had been brought about because teachers expected them to misbehave based on their past behaviour, or sometimes even on the behaviour of an older sibling. Fairness was an important principle for young people. They believed they were sometimes the victims of deliberate, highly subjective and even whimsical judgements leading to their exclusion. Professionals argue against a strict tariff system for exclusions because the rigidity of that system would limit their scope for considering all of the circumstances of the pupil's life at the time of the incident. This is a strong argument but there was no evidence that it was appreciated by pupils – they saw differences as unfair rather than as appropriate to individual circumstances.

Munn and Lloyd (2005) also note that excluded pupils sometimes saw themselves as the agents of their own exclusion and demonstrated a tendency to individualise problems and see them as private troubles (2005: 213). This was not the case for a number of pupils in this study who saw themselves as the agents of their own exclusion but they valorised their actions as asserting their right to be treated respectfully by teachers. For pupils, their agency had a social purpose and was related to their negotiations of particular kinds of identity. School staff, on the other hand, was more likely to attribute exclusions to individual or private difficulties. This contrast again illustrates how pupils sometimes resisted the label, or the identity, schools attempted to construct for them, especially where that label was demeaning. Social interactionists have argued that for someone to be successfully 'typed' or labeled, s/he had to cooperate in accepting the label. Gender theorists (Connell, 1995; 2002; Francis and Skelton, 2001; Francis, 2005) offered a more developed view whereby identities were fluid, layered and subject to ongoing negotiations in school settings and elsewhere. In resisting attempts to pathologise their behaviour, pupils were negotiating identities more powerful and attractive than those offered by the school. By attributing behaviour difficulties to pupils' individual and personal troubles, teachers would see themselves as embodying a 'welfare approach' to young people, rather than a wholly punitive one. Parsons (2005: 199) argues that a genuine support-based, nurturing approach is 'aspirational' only without a global redistribution of wealth. Most approaches to challenging behaviour in his view embody 'a third way' approach, combining individual and structural solutions. Even those attempts to label which were well-intentioned could deny agency to pupils themselves.

Power is distributed and withheld in school communities in ways which minimise participation for some within the school community. Schooling does not generally involve pupils in 'naming the world' (Freire, 1970). Pupils are not actively engaged in the web of social relations through which common understandings are constructed and shared values are formed. They tend to be on the receiving end, rather than the formative end, of the judgements which matter. Schools allow very little control to pupils, in part because they are seen to be children and also because schools are traditionally very hierarchical and authoritarian. For pupils such as Andy and Ross, who were organising their own lives, school seemed to be challenging their self-determination and exerted over them what Willis (1978) called 'an unjustified authority'. Excluded pupils may be seen as exercising agency, therefore, in the conscious and continuing challenge they present to the authority of the school. This challenge is part of a process of negotiation of particular kinds of masculine identities; 'the relationships constructing masculinity are dialectical; they do not correspond to the one-way causation of a socialization model' (Connell, 1995: 37).

Schools could do more to recognise the dialectic involved in processes of identity negotiation by increasing opportunities for pupil participation. This would help to avoid the attribution of labels unwelcome to young women and young men. This point is pursued further on.

But the class and gendered subjectivities of boys and girls were formed beyond school, too, and were sustained and further developed through conflict with school norms. Habitus was demonstrated in their anti-school behaviour and in their exclusion. The particular circumstances of their lives shaped their relationship with schooling, and changed it as they grew older and their awareness of those circumstances increased. For a number of the case study pupils, schooling was perceived to be irrelevant to the lives they were leading and were likely to lead in the future. They and their families were ill-placed to engage with schooling in ways helpful to their attainment and to their life chances. Pupils in this study were engaged in the active negotiation of gender and class identities and to that extent they exercised agency. The range of identities open to pupils was set by structural factors, by the economic circumstances of their lives. Indications came from schools of their limited influence over the lives of pupils, as was sometimes expressed by school staff. 'Sometimes they are a bit of an enigma to me . . . all these boys actually, I would say that all of them are probably bright enough to play their future out so differently, but they just can't' (Behaviour support teacher).

The next section will consider the implications of these discussions for policy and for school practices.

Policy implications

Social justice in education is challenged by evidence from this study and others (Munn *et al.* 2000; Parsons, 1999). Can school provision be developed in ways that reduce exclusion? The final section of this chapter will consider what this means for policy and school provision. The problem for schools will be outlined and set against the wider problem schools cause by excluding some pupils.

School exclusion and social exclusion

School exclusions present a dilemma for social policy in Scotland. Exclusion was noted as serving only one purpose for 20 per cent pupils repeatedly excluded in any one year; it protected learning and teaching in the classroom for teachers and other pupils. From classroom observation and from interviews with staff and pupils, there was considerable evidence that the behaviour of some pupils was undermining of teaching and learning. The exclusion of those pupils was indeed helpful to the calm functioning of classrooms. Teachers' views of exclusions varied slightly from the official view here in that they saw exclusions as not just ensuring continuity of learning and teaching but also as providing respite from the hostile and sometimes highly abusive behaviour of some pupils. Those repeatedly excluded were working-class children living in poverty. Along with their families, they experienced the emotional, social and physical stresses of poverty, as well as its material deprivations. Those circumstances affected their engagement with schooling and contributed to their repeated exclusion. In turn, their exclusion undermined their education, compounding their social marginalisation for the present and into the future.

Attempts to break this cycle have come from school policy initiatives and broader social policy. Through a welter of initiatives under banners such as *Better Behaviour – Better Learning* (SEED, 2000a) and *Getting it Right for Every Child* (Scottish Government, 2008), schools have addressed the development of school and classroom ethos, with some success in reducing challenging behaviour and exclusions. For example, one issue raised by classroom disruption was teachers' skills in managing behaviour; the same group of pupils may work purposefully with one teacher while creating havoc with another teacher. Staff development and implementation of behaviour management packages may help teachers to improve their skills. Such measure went only so far in the view of professionals interviewed. There were behaviours that were not caused by school factors, nor were those behaviours susceptible to school remedies. Schools had moved some way to improving provision and practice but school improvement in itself was seen to address neither the causes nor the symptoms of some very challenging behaviours.

Social inclusion policy and school policy have recognised the difficulties of some groups in engaging with mainstream services. In education, initiatives such as the *New Community Schools* (SOEID, 1998b) roll-out and, more recently, *Schools of Ambition* (SEED, 2004) have tried to foster the educational prospects of marginalised groups. From evaluative studies (Munn *et al.* 2004), there were indications that additional staffing provided under *Better Behaviour – Better Learning* funding was helpful to some of the young people, especially where that staffing related to the whole experience of young people. Home/school link workers, in particular, had gained the trust and confidence of some of the case study pupils who were experiencing greatest difficulty in their home lives. As a result of the support they received, young people were perhaps less angry and brittle in school settings, more able to deal with the stresses of their lives, and had access to an adult who could mediate on their behalf with the school. While this helped maintain pupils' connection to schooling, and reduced exclusions, it did not assist with their participation in the curriculum. Learning within the curriculum is the core function of schooling, providing among other things the credentials necessary for young people to make successful transitions to work and wider social participation. Retaining children on the margins of schooling is better than allowing them to become detached altogether but it will not equip them for a future away from the periphery of society.

Some commentators have detected a 'welfare' approach to challenging behaviour rather than a punitive approach (Parsons, 2005; MacLeod and Munn, 2004) in some anti-exclusion policy initiatives. Such approaches may be stigmatising of families (Millbourne, 2002) and have no impact on the wider context causing their social exclusion in the first place (Riddell and Tett, 2001; Whitty, 2001; Macrae *et al.* 2003). There was evidence in this study that case study pupils did not welcome 'welfare' approaches from teachers, preferring conflict and exclusion. Their negotiation of working-class, masculine identities, in particular, precluded their acceptance of labels demeaning to them. They and their families were not well positioned in relation to education because of wider structural inequalities. The social inclusion initiatives they experienced were not intended to tackle those inequalities and were seen in this study to be capable of supporting pupils on the margins but not of moving them into the mainstream processes of schooling.

Policy initiatives to reduce exclusion

Social policy has targeted, sometimes literally, a reduction in school exclusions and schools have developed a number of strategies to achieve that end. One such strategy has been the development of stronger systems of behaviour support, sometimes in the form of bases or units within the mainstream school (Head *et al.* 2003, Kane *et al.* 2004). Behaviour support bases in secondary schools have been used flexibly for a number of purposes but have sometimes been used as means of reducing exclusions by enabling 'internal exclusion' (Munn *et al.* 1997). In addition, schools have been criticised for under-reporting exclusions (Munn *et al.* 2000) and there was further evidence here that this is, indeed, the case. For example, Craig's exclusions seemed not always to be recorded. In primary school he was sent home a few times but this was not 'suspended' as such: 'They just called it a cooling-off period or something' (Craig).

Schools were very open about their use of the 'sending home' mechanism whereby pupils were sent away with a letter home and told to return only when their parent could come to the school to discuss matters. Schools' frankness here suggests that they saw this tack as a means of managing responsibly fraught situations, of defusing conflict and preventing exclusion and not just as a means of massaging exclusion statistics. The monitoring of numbers of exclusions was viewed by schools as framed by the school improvement discourse (rather than a social justice discourse) and, as with the monitoring of attainment through Scottish Qualifications Agency data, there was scepticism that this exercise (even without the target-setting dimension) could assist the capacity of schools to provide well for young people. In fact, in their openness about sending pupils home, schools seemed to see themselves as setting their care/welfare responsibilities against their accountability function in terms of reporting exclusions.

Behaviour support in the four secondary schools in this study was much more refined than simply a means of 'internal exclusions'. Again and again in interviews, school staff spoke of their desire for flexibility to accommodate the range of pupil needs. Since the Warnock Report (DES, 1978), and the Her Majesty's Inspectorate (HMI) Progress Report in Scotland (SED, 1978), this flexibility has been in terms of the curriculum with differentiated approaches taking all pupils towards the same broad educational aims. Indeed, in the 1990s, the 5–14 initiative in Scotland was heralded as offering the Scottish system, for the first time, an inclusive curricular framework. New curriculum guidelines, *Curriculum for Excellence* (Scottish Executive, 2004), will similarly frame the education of all children. Some have argued that this framework provides all the inclusion that is needed, with special and mainstream schools continuing to operate in parallel towards the same goals. There is evidence emerging from schools to suggest that this concensus around the common goals of education is breaking down. Schools are again looking for 'alternative curricula' and perceptions of the relevance of education to the prospective lives of young people is taking schools towards very functional, skills-based curriculum packages for some children (Dyson, 2001). Support structures left pupils still on the margins of schooling, attached but not involved. Greater flexibility of provision for all pupils is likely to help as are much stronger attempts to engage pupils, families and communities in articulating the purposes of schooling and in designing curricular paths related to those purposes.

There was evidence from key informant interviews that schools' attempts to avoid the exclusion of some young people had led them to patronise alternative forms of provision beyond the school sector, for example, provision offered by the further education sector and by private providers traditionally associated with post-compulsory and vocational education. A senior education officer noted that this practice was an expensive drain on public resources. In addition, the coherence of provision was not quality assured and supported through, for example, systems of joint staff development. The symbolic importance of these practices outweighs pragmatic considerations – they reveal not only individual schools but the school system itself to be shedding responsibility for some pupils. The impetus for schools to build their own inclusive capacity had been made explicit in *Better Behaviour – Better Learning* (SEED, 2000a) but, nevertheless, schools in areas with high levels of social exclusion were reported as seeking solutions elsewhere. This would seem to indicate an abandonment of some of the principles of inclusion and breadth of access which have been pursued for decades in Scottish education. Inclusion is constructed as education which is relevant to the current circumstances of the pupil rather than appropriate to their higher aspirations. Rather than schools enabling upward social mobility in Scottish society, the practice pointed to schools educating some children for a life of exclusion.

Exclusion is the effect rather than the intention of school policy, particularly with regard to raising attainment. The tension between the policy priorities of inclusion and raising attainment have been noted by some commentators (Parsons, 1999; Cooper *et al.* 2000) as contributing to rising rates of school exclusion. Clark *et al.* (1998) set this particular conflict in priorities in a broader incompatibility in the purposes of schooling between, for example, the achievement of equity alongside the maximising of individual achievement and the development of the nation's economic infrastructure (Clark *et al.* 1998: 167). Through empirical studies, commentators (Florian and Rouse, 2001) have explored whether inclusion and raising attainment are mutually exclusive and have found this to be not necessarily the case. Evidence emerged in this study, too, of classrooms where cooperative teaching was used to great effect in ensuring the learning of all pupils, including one case study pupil who was observed to be very disruptive in another lesson. School staff in this study reported difficulty in pursuing both priorities simultaneously, especially when raising attainment was linked to academic targets. Respondents emphasised the purpose of exclusions as to protect ongoing learning and teaching and suggested that some of the pressures felt by teachers (and communicated to pupils) to ensure coverage of the curriculum resulted in a less tolerant approach to distraction. In the drive to raise attainment, those who were perceived to counter the school's efforts could be excluded in a variety of ways, including self-exclusion, segregation in a base or attendance at provision apart from formal school settings. With regard to raising attainment in this study, there was an indication that parents and young people were selecting schools according to their image as either 'inclusive' or 'strict'. The key informant boys interviewed suggested that the two local secondary schools had very different images in the community, so much so that parents would cross the denominational divide and split siblings to try to gain schooling appropriate to their child's needs. This suggests that, at least in the perception of the community, schools are choosing to prioritise academic attainment or supportive/inclusive practices. In some communities, there would seem to be a danger of a bipartite system of education emerging.

Development of policy and provision

Study of class and gender identities, the means by which they are negotiated in and beyond school settings, and the structural limits to those negotiations, can offer insights into the disproportionate exclusion of some groups. What do those insights mean for how school provision is developed? There is an extensive literature on the development of inclusive schooling (for example, Thomas and Loxley, 2001; Skidmore, 2004; Thomas and Vaughan, 2004; Lewis and Norwich, 2005; Rix *et al.* 2005), particularly on the development of inclusive schooling for pupils with Special Educational Needs/Additional Support Need (SEN/ASN). That body of literature has been extended to encompass inclusion as it pertains to socially excluded pupils (Whitty, 2001; Dyson, 2001). Discussion of inclusive approaches for pupils with SEN/ASN has focused recently on pedagogies to support classroom inclusion (Lewis and Norwich, 2005; Davis and Florian, 2004). This study did not contribute to that aspect of the inclusion debate although there was a startling contrast in the behaviour of one case study boy between two different lessons, indicating the importance of teachers' values and commitment to inclusive pedagogies in ensuring positive experiences of schooling. This is not to argue that the development of pedagogies will in itself prevent exclusion in all or even most cases. The argument here is that some pupils are negotiating particular identities through individual and collective opposition to schooling and that those negotiations relate to lives beyond schooling. Some pupils in this study behaved very badly: their presence in school made life very difficult for teachers and sometimes for other pupils. They present a substantial challenge to advocates of inclusive schooling. At the moment, the solution for schools is to discard those pupils through repeated and ever-lengthening exclusions. This practice is incompatible with a commitment to social justice in the education system and so there is an imperative towards their inclusion. This is not to suggest a utopian vision of school inclusion whereby intractable educational problems related to structural inequality might be resolved. In pursuit of equity, though, development of school provision may be helpful for some pupils.

How can schools respond to the disengagement of some pupils, mainly working-class boys? In this study some boys were given space to move away from the peer group by setting and streaming but for many others, those organisational practices consolidated their disengagement from schooling. Other strategies used by schools to address gender inequalities were underpinned by the misguided notion that masculinity is one-dimensional, inherent and static. Munn and Lloyd (2005) argue that schools can promote inclusion by tackling the strong sense coming from excluded pupils that teachers do not listen, do not treat pupils with respect, and do not behave fairly. Approaches drawn from Restorative Justice (Hopkins, 2004; Hendry, 2009) have been seen to offer a means of creating more positive school cultures, offering a challenge to the 'control paradigm', which emphasises arbitrary authority over pupil participation (Cameron and Thorsborne, 2001: 8). A range of practices are termed 'Restorative', for example, Circle Time, peer-mediation, as well as more formal techniques such as conferencing where the aim is to address specific incidents causing hurt or harm to people and relationships. Evidence suggests that the imperative towards punishment is reduced where schools emphasise the importance of maintaining and restoring relationships in the school community (McCluskey *et al.* 2008; Kane *et al.* 2009).

Excluded pupils in this study expressed the view that they were treated unfairly and that teachers did not listen to them but they also had contrasting experiences of other members of staff, some of whom were teachers. Where there were mutually respectful relationships between pupils and a member of staff, a very valuable point of contact with schooling was created for pupils who were otherwise rapidly disengaging. The rigid organisation of secondary schooling prevented the maximum opportunity being made of those positive relationships. In pursuit of increased flexibility, schools have developed much stronger systems of pupil support, including behaviour support. In the case study schools, there were well developed and sometimes highly individualised systems of pupil support. However, as pupils spent more and more time in behaviour support classes and bases, their curriculum shifted towards personal and social development (PSD), counselling and anger management. Some had cause to be angry and anger management was helpful to them but it was usually provided at the expense of an academic curriculum, even where pupils had high levels of ability in the subjects they missed. In those circumstances, subject teachers sometimes expressed their sense of the unfairness to pupils.

The flexibility offered by systems of behaviour support has been helpful for schools but it has also increased their capacity for curricular exclusion. More flexible ways of organising the curriculum could help pupils to make the most of positive connections some had. An increasingly prescribed curriculum has become ever more prescribed. A core plus options curricular structure, separated out from age and stage correspondences, would enable all pupils to spend more time in areas where they were doing well and where their motivations were higher. According greater scope to pupils and families generally in planning their curriculum would also be consistent with increasing their participation in schooling. Within such a structure, behaviour support could become itself less marginalised if it fulfilled a curricular planning role for some pupils within a broader system of pupil support. Dyson *et al.* (2003) reviewed the literature on school inclusion and identified the need for schools to build close relations with parents and communities based on developing a shared commitment to inclusive values. The study offered some insight into how school organisation might be developed to allow greater participation of parents. Progress towards a new single curriculum framework in Scotland, *Curriculum for Excellence* (Scottish Executive, 2004), offers an opportunity to enable greater choice and flexibility within the curriculum and thereby increase the participation in schooling of pupils and families.

Chapter 8

Conclusion

Exclusion from school was a starting point here for considering the experiences of those who were excluded but the practice of exclusion itself raised issues about schooling in secondary schools. Many of the case study samples were already experiencing exclusionary processes, apart from their formal exclusion. Those processes were tied up with constructions of 'ability'. Even where pupils had previously been noted as very bright, their perceived lack of motivation as they grew older caused them to be placed in lower-ability groups, compounding their oppositional attitudes and further alienating them from schooling.

Within those broad exclusionary processes, three further forms of pupil exclusion were found. Truancy is a form of self-exclusion from the school system for girls and boys because they appear to be choosing to withdraw from participation in schooling. Pupils making that choice exercised limited agency; structural factors such as poverty shaped pupils' engagement with schooling and increased the barriers to participation. The second form of unofficial exclusion was informal exclusion, that is, unrecorded exclusion. Informal exclusions occurred when pupils were sent home from school, ostensibly to provide a 'cooling off' period for the pupil and others involved in conflict, and pending discussions with the pupil's parents. Such exclusions are not recorded and it has been suggested that they are prompted less by concern for pupils' and teachers' composure than by schools' desire to demonstrate low rates of exclusion in official returns. The 'sending home' mechanism disadvantaged young people whose families were unable to respond quickly. Pupils were out of school, recorded as absent, until their parent returned with them. The third type of unofficial exclusion is 'internal' exclusion where in-school units or bases are used as an alternative to formal exclusion. Pupils presenting challenging behaviour are sent to the unit or base for all or some of their schooling over a varying period of time. Provision in behaviour support bases differs, sometimes offering pupils constructive educational opportunities while at other times serving a holding or even a punitive, 'sin bin' function for pupils judged to be disruptive of ordinary. These three forms of unofficial exclusion are linked to each other and to official exclusions. For example, the practice of sending pupils home on an informal basis, or to a behaviour support base, is used as a low-tariff response leading to higher-tariff, formal exclusion. Pupils who are formally excluded will often have previous experience of 'internal' or informal exclusion and, especially after S3, will be more likely to withdraw from schooling for all or part of the time. School exclusions peak in S3, one year before the end of compulsory schooling, and this pattern has been linked to the self-exclusion of pupils who have previously been formally excluded.

Exclusions were noted by key informants as having a range of purposes but the official view was that there were just two: to deter bad behaviour in future and to protect learning and teaching in classrooms. The former purpose was said to serve excluded pupils in deterring them from future wrongdoing but statistics revealed that some 20 per cent of excluded pupils had been repeatedly excluded and there was some scepticism among school-based key informants as to the deterrent value of exclusions. The pointers were that the over-riding purpose of exclusion was the latter purpose cited by officials – to protect learning and teaching for teachers and the majority of pupils. In other words, exclusion had no benefit for the excluded pupil. This is understandable where some pupils were undermining learning and teaching but questions of social justice in education are raised when approximately 4,000 pupils per year are repeatedly excluded from Scottish schools. Exclusion, especially repeated exclusion, increased existing social disadvantage by undermining the education of mainly working-class boys and could be seen as representing a much wider alienation of the working-class from education.

Exclusion was at odds with policy priorities in education relating to inclusion and to the targeting of support towards children and young people seen to be vulnerable. Exclusion did not relate to those official discourses of inclusion but the practice of exclusion did resonate with particular discourses of social exclusion. Media accounts of indiscipline drew on a 'moral underclass' view where poverty and disadvantage generally were pathologised, seen as attributable to the fecklessness and lack of control of individuals. By that account, school exclusions and broader social exclusion could be seen as punishment for failure to seize the opportunities made available. Young people and their families experienced exclusion as a punishment.

Statistics showed patterns of exclusion were strongly structured by gender and social class. Anti-school behaviour among secondary-aged boys has been explained in terms of their need to develop the collective resistance important to their future lives labouring in industrial capitalism. Those futures were no longer available but girls' and boys' behaviour was seen still to be hostile to schooling. In many cases, their interactions with schooling were fraught and difficult. The transitions they faced were not assisted by schools which tended to focus efforts only on transition to higher education. Young people were aware of the difficulties they faced and some of them took responsibility for managing their futures themselves, for example, in deciding to join the army or to use contacts to find work. Although, they would sort out their futures on an individual basis, collective identities were highly valued with girls and boys using features such as dress and dialect, and their sense of belonging to particular localities, to denote and sustain cultural commonality. Exclusion can be very bonding for those excluded; social exclusion itself seemed to have fostered collective identities. The economic circumstances of pupils' lives and the identities they negotiated within those circumstances tied up with their exclusion from school and with broader working-class experience of education. Although pupils exercised agency in the processes leading to their exclusion, that agency was heavily circumscribed by the economic, social and cultural circumstances of their lives.

Repeated experience of school exclusion was seen to undermine and sometimes destroy pupils' participation in schooling and to deny them the benefits accruing from education and formal credentials. The manner in which exclusions are reduced is such that pupils are usually left still on the margins of schooling, attached but not involved. School approaches to tackling exclusion would require greater flexibility of provision for all pupils and much stronger attempts to engage pupils, families and communities in articulating the purposes of schooling and in designing curricular paths related to those purposes. This would provide a more consistent and a more committed attempt to address social exclusion but still seems unlikely to solve the problem. Structural factors such as poverty and inequality have been identified as a main cause of exclusion requiring a political commitment. To lift children out of exclusion and marginalisation within schooling, families and communities have to be lifted out of relative poverty.

Appendix 1

School exclusions in Scotland

In Scotland, exclusions are governed by Scottish Executive Circular No. 8/03 (SEED, 2003) which sets out procedures and requirements for administering and reporting exclusions. Exclusions are the most serious of the sanctions used by schools to punish those pupils who break the behaviour code of the school. Two categories of exclusion, temporary exclusion and 'removed from the register' (of the current school), are recognised in the regulations governing school exclusions (Schools General [Scotland] Regulations, 1975). The period of exclusion for particular kinds of misbehaviour is not prescribed but local authorities (LAs) usually place a ceiling of 20 school days on the term of the exclusion, with pupils being asked to leave the school for a period of between two days and four weeks depending upon the nature of the incident. Schools would usually develop their own 'tariff' system where offences judged to be less serious, or first misdemeanours, would be punished with periods of up to three days. The tariff would usually rise on each subsequent occasion if the pupil were judged to have again breached the disciplinary code. The lack of regulation of the period of exclusions leads to inequities with the same or similar 'offence' attracting widely differing punishments depending upon the school, the pupil, the teachers involved and other factors. While this situation leads to unfairness, it is also seen (by professionals) as having a positive side, as it allows schools to respond flexibly and in ways which take account of factors such as the personal circumstances of the pupil, as well as the seriousness of the disciplinary incident. Scottish Executive Education Department (SEED) guidelines endorse the use of professional judgement: 'Education authorities and schools, when deciding whether exclusion is necessary, must have regard to the particular facts and circumstances surrounding individual incidents and/or pupils' (SEED, 2003: sec. 2.10).

The second type of exclusion practised in Scotland – 'removed from the register' of the school – is utilised where the offence is regarded as serious, or where a particular pupil has had a number of previous temporary exclusions for earlier breaches of the code. In such cases and within the four-week period of the exclusion, the headteacher of the school would be invited to attend a meeting with representatives of the education authority, the pupil, his/her parents and their representatives so that the school placement offered to the pupil might be considered in a welfare as well as a disciplinary light. In spite of the intention to make the interests of the pupil central to the decision about placement, the process sometimes breaks down at this point, for example, when the alternative placement offered to the pupil and his family is unacceptable to them for reasons of distance from the family home. Pupils can therefore be out of the school system for much longer than the period of the original exclusion. The regulations in Scotland differ from those in England where three types of exclusion are practised – 'fixed-term' (similar to 'temporary' discussed earlier), 'indefinite' and 'permanent'.

Appendix 2

Type and range of data for each case study

Key to abbreviations overleaf

CSP	Interview with case study pupil
T1, etc.	Interview with subject teacher
BS	Interview with behaviour support teacher
SMT	Interview with member of senior management team (HT, DHT or AHT)
Par	Interview with parent/carer of case study pupil
Ob1, etc.	Episode of classroom observation
Rec	Study of school's behaviour records/files

Carrick High School

Table 1 Case study overview: Carrick High School

		CSP	T1	T2	Ob 1	Ob 2	SMT	H/S	Par	Rec
Ross	S1	✓	✓		✓		✓	✓		✓
Dougie	S3	✓	✓	✓			✓	✓		✓
Jim	S1	✓	✓		✓		✓			✓
Jack	S3	✓	✓		✓		✓			✓
Billy	S1	✓	✓		✓		✓			✓

General

- interviews and focus groups in school with pupils from classes of case study pupils
- interview with SMT person regarding policy in school
- documents (handbook, policies, etc.) collected from school
- attendance and exclusion statistics for case study pupils collected.

Easton High School

Table 2 Case study overview: Easton High School

		CSP	T1	T2	Ob 1	Ob 2	SMT	H/S	Par	Rec
Alan	S3	✓	✓				✓			✓
Lorraine	S3	✓	✓	✓	✓	✓	✓	✓		✓
Sam	S2	✓	✓	✓	✓	✓	✓	✓	✓	✓
Gary	S2	✓	✓	✓	✓	✓	✓	✓	✓	✓
Joe	S2	✓					✓			✓

General

- interviews and focus groups in school with pupils from classes of case study pupils
- interview with SMT person regarding policy in school
- documents (handbook, policies, etc.) collected from school
- attendance and exclusion statistics for case study pupils collected.

St Thomas's High School

Table 3 Case study overview: St Thomas's High School

		CSP	T1	T2	T3	Ob 1	Ob 2	SMT	H/S	BS	Par	Rec
Ewen	S3	✓	✓	✓	✓	✓	✓	✓		✓		
Charlie	S3	✓	✓	✓	✓	✓	✓	✓		✓		
Eddie	S3	✓	✓	✓	✓	✓		✓		✓		
Kat	S3	✓	✓	✓	✓	✓	✓	✓		✓		

General

- interview with SMT person regarding policy in school
- documents (handbook, policies, etc.) collected from school
- attendance and exclusion statistics for case study pupils collected.

Hammond High School

Table 4 Case study overview: Hammond High School

		CSP	T1	T2	T3	Ob 1	Ob 2	SMT	BS	Par	Rec
Davy	S3	✓	✓	✓		✓	✓	✓	✓		✓
Andy	S2	✓	✓	✓	✓	✓	✓	✓	✓		✓
Craig	S2	✓	✓	✓	✓	✓		✓	✓		✓
Maz	S3	✓	✓			✓	✓	✓	✓		✓
Gill	S3	✓	✓	✓	✓				✓		✓
Baz	S3	✓	✓	✓	✓	✓		✓	✓		✓

General

- interview with SMT person regarding policy in school
- documents (handbook, policies, etc.) collected from school
- attendance and exclusion statistics for case study pupils collected.

Bibliography

Ainscow, M. (1993) *Towards Effective Schools for All*, National Association for Special Educational Needs.
Allan, J. (2008) *Re-thinking Inclusive Education: the philosophers of difference in practice*, Dordrecht, Springer.
Alvey, S. and Brown, U. (2001) *Social Exclusion: briefing sheet 13*, Glasgow, Scottish Poverty Information Unit.
Archer, L. and Yamashita, H. (2003) 'Theorising Inner-city Masculinities: "race", class, gender and education', *Gender and Education*, 15: 2: 115–32.
Arnot, M. (2002) *Reproducing Gender? Essays on educational theory and feminist politics*, London, RoutledgeFalmer.
— (2003) 'Male Working-class Identities and Social Justice: a reconsideration of Paul Willis's learning to labour in light of contemporary research'. In Vincent, C. (ed.) *Social Justice, Education and Identity*, London, RoutledgeFalmer.
Ball, S. (1981) *Beachside Comprehensive*, Cambridge, Cambridge University Press.
— (2003) *Class Strategies and the Educational Market: the middle classes and social advantage*, London, RoutledgeFalmer.
— (2006) *Education Policy and Social Class*, London, Routledge.
Barratt, C. (2009) *Trade Union Membership 2008*, London, National Statistics Publication: http://stats.berr.gov.uk/UKSA/tu/tum2008.pdf. Accessed 13 January 2010.
Beck, U. (1992) *Risk Society*, London, Sage.
Black-Hawkins, K., Florian, L. and Rouse, M. (2007) *Achievement and Inclusion in Schools*, London, RoutledgeFalmer.
Blyth, E. and Milner, J. (1996) 'Black Boys Excluded from School: race or masculinity issues? in Blyth, E. and Milner, J. (eds) *Exclusions From School: interprofessional issues for policy and practice*, London, Routledge.
Booth, T., Ainscow, M., Black-Hawkins, K., Vaughan, M. and Shaw, L. (2000) *Index for Inclusion: developing learning and participation in schools*, Bristol, Centre for Studies in Inclusive Education.
Bourdieu, P. (1990) *The Logic of Practice*, Cambridge, Polity Press.
Bourdieu, P. and Wacquant, L. (1992) *An Invitation to Reflexive Sociology*, Chicago, University of Chicago Press.
Boyd, B. (2007) 'Family Support: educational achievement and social exclusion', *Education in the North*, 15: 23–31.
Broadfoot, P. (1996) *Education, Assessment and Society: a sociological analysis*, Buckingham, Open University Press.
Brown, J. (2005) '"Violent Girls": same or different from "other" girls?' In Lloyd, G. (ed.) *Problem*

Girls: understanding and supporting troubled and troublesome girls and young women, London, RoutledgeFalmer.
Brown, M. J. and Gilligan, C. (1992) *Meeting at the Crossroads: women's psychology and girls' development*, Cambridge, MA, Harvard University Press.
Bynner, J., Chisholm, L. and Furlong, A. (1998) *Youth Citizenship and Social Change in a European Context*, Aldershot, Ashgate.
Cameron, L. and Thorsborne, M. (2001) 'Restorative Justice and School Discipline: mutually exclusive?' In Strang, H. and Braithwaite, J. (eds) *Restorative Justice and Civil Society*, Cambridge, Cambridge University Press, 180–94.
Caulfield, C. and Hill, M. (2002) *The Experience of Black and Minority Ethnic Young People Following the Transition to Secondary School*, Glasgow, Scottish Council for Research in Education.
Clark, C., Dyson, A. and Millward, A. (1998) *Theorising Special Education*, London, Routledge.
Cogan, N. (2004) *Young Carers of Parents with Mental Health Problems*, PhD thesis, University of Glasgow.
Connell, R. W. (1989) 'Cool Guys, Swots and Wimps: the interplay of masculinities and education', *Oxford Review of Education*, 15: 3: 291–303.
— (1995) *Masculinities*, Cambridge, Polity Press.
— (2002) *Gender*, Cambridge, Polity Press.
Cooper, P., Hart, S., Lovey, J. and McLaughlin, C. (2000) *Positive Alternatives to Exclusion from School*, London, Routledge.
Davis, P. and Florian, L. (2004) *Teaching Strategies and Approaches for Pupils with Special Educational Needs: a scoping study*, London, DfES.
Department of Education and Science (DES) (1978) *Special Educational Needs: The Warnock Report*, London, HMSO.
Devine, T. M. (2000) *Scotland's Shame: bigotry and sectarianism in modern Scotland*, Edinburgh, Mainstream Publishing.
DiGeorgio, C. (2009) 'Application of Bourdieuian Theory to the Inclusion of Students with Learning/Physical Challenges in Multicultural School Settings', *International Journal of Inclusive Education*, 13: 2: 179–94.
Dyson, A. (2001) 'Special Needs in the Twenty-first Century: where we've been and where we're going', *British Journal of Special Education*, 28: 1: 24–29.
Dyson, A., Howes, A. and Roberts, B. (2003) *What Do We Really Know About Inclusive Schools? A systematic review of the research evidence*, Paper to AERA, Chicago, April, 2003.
Epstein, D. (1997) 'Boyz, Own Stories: masculinities and sexualities in schools', *Gender and Education*, 9: 1: 105–15.
— (1998) 'Real Boys don't Work: "underachievement", masculinity and the harassment of "sissies"'. In Epstein, D., Elwood, J., Hey, V. and Maw, J. (eds) *Failing Boys? Issues in gender and achievement*, Buckingham, Open University Press.
Esping-Andersen, G. (1990) *The Three Worlds of Welfare Capitalism*, Cambridge, Polity Press.
Evans, K. and Furlong, A. (1997) 'Metaphors of Youth Transitions: niches, pathways, trajectories or navigations'. In Bynner, J., Chisholm, L. and Furlong, A. (eds) (1998) *Youth Citizenship and Social Change in a European Context*, Aldershot, Ashgate.
Florian, L. and Kershner, R. (2009) 'Inclusive Pedagogy'. In Daniels, H., Lauder, H. and Porter, J. (eds) *Knowledge, Values and Educational Policy: a critical perspective*, London, Routledge.
Florian, L. and Rouse, M. (2001) 'Inclusive Practice in English Secondary Schools: lessons learned', *Cambridge Journal of Education*, 31: 2: 399–412.
Francis, B. (2000) *Boys, Girls and Achievement: addressing the classroom issues*, London, RoutledgeFalmer.

— (2005) 'Not/Knowing their Place: girls classroom behaviour'. In Lloyd, G. (Ed) *Problem Girls: understanding and supporting troubled and troublesome girls and young women*, London, RoutledgeFalmer.
Francis, B. and Skelton, C. (2001) *Investigating Gender: contemporary perspectives in education*, Buckingham, Open University Press.
Frank, B., Kehler, M., Lovell, T. and Davison, K. (2003) 'A Tangle of Trouble: boys, masculinities and schooling – future directions', *Educational Review*, 55: 2: 119–33.
Fraser, N. (1997) *Justice Interruptus: critical reflections on the 'postsocialist' condition*, London, Routledge.
Freire, P. (1970) *The Pedagogy of the Oppressed*, London, Penguin.
Furlong, A. and Cartmel, F. (1997) *Young People and Social Change: individualization and risk in late modernity*, Buckingham, Open University Press.
— (2007) (2nd edn) *Young People and Social Change: new perspectives*, Maidenhead, Open University Press.
Furlong, V. J. (1985) *The Deviant Pupil: sociological perpectives*, Milton Keynes, Open University Press.
Garland, D. (2001). *The Culture of Control*, Oxford, Oxford University Press.
Giddens, A. (1990) *The Consequences of Modernity*, Cambridge, Polity Press.
Gormley, N. (2003) *Excluded Youth: what works? A review of practice in tackling youth exclusion*, Edinburgh, Scottish Executive.
Granville, S., Staniforth, J. and Clapton, R. (2006) *Investigating Local Authority Procedures for Identifying and Registering Children Eligible for Free School Meal Entitlement*, Edinburgh, Scottish Executive.
Gray, J., Hopkins, D., Reynolds, D., Wilcox, B., Farrell, S. and Jesson, D. (1999) *Improving Schools: performance and potential*, Buckingham, Open University Press.
Hamilton, L. (2002) 'Constructing Pupil Identity: personhood and ability', *British Educational Research Journal*, 28: 4: 591–602.
Hanafin, J. and Lynch, A. (2002) 'Peripheral Voices, Parental Involvement, Social Class and Educational Disadvantage', *British Journal of Sociology of Education*, 23:1: 35–49.
Hargreaves, D. (1967) *Social Relations in a Secondary School*, London, Routledge and Kegan Paul.
Hayden, C. (1997) *Children Excluded from Primary School: debates, evidence, responses*, Buckingham, Open University Press.
Haywood, C. and Mac an Ghaill, M. (2006) 'Education and Gender Identity: seeking frameworks of understanding'. In M. Arnot and Mac an Ghaill, M. (eds) *The RoutledgeFalmer Reader in Gender and Education*, London, Routledge.
Head, G., Kane, J. and Cogan, N. (2003) 'Behaviour Support in Secondary Schools: what works for schools?' *Emotional and Behavioural Difficulties*, 8: 1: 33–42.
Hendry, R. (2009) *Building and Restoring Respectful Relationships in School: a guide to using restorative practice*, London, Routledge.
Hopkins, B. (2004) *Just Schools: a whole school approach to restorative justice*, London, Jessica Kingsley.
Howieson, C. and Ianelli, C. (2008) 'The Effects of Low Attainment on Young People's Outcomes at Age 22–23', *British Educational Research Journal*, 34: 2: 269–90.
Ingram, N. (2009) 'Working-class Boys, Educational Success and the Misrecognition of Working-class Culture', *British Journal of Sociology of Education*, 30: 4: 421–34.
Jackson, C. (2002) '"Laddishness" as a Self-worth Protection Strategy', *Gender and Education*, 14: 1: 37–51.

— (2006a) '"Wild" girls? An exploration of "ladette" cultures in secondary schools', *Gender and Education*, 18: 4: 339–60.
— (2006b) *Lads and Ladettes in School: gender and a fear of failure*, Maidenhead, Open University Press.
Kane, J., Head, G. and Cogan, N. (2004) 'Towards Inclusion? Models of behaviour support in secondary schools in one local authority in Scotland', *British Journal of Special Education*, 31: 2: 68–74.
Kane, J., Lloyd, G., McCluskey, G., Maguire, R., Riddell, S., Stead, J. and Weedon, E. (2009) 'Generating an Inclusive Ethos? Exploring the impact of restorative practices in Scottish schools international', *Journal of Inclusive Education*, 13: 3: 231–52.
Kenway, J. and Fitzclarence, L. (1997) 'Masculinity, Violence and Schooling: challenging poisonous pedagogies', *Gender and Education*, 9 (Special issue on masculinities): 117–33.
Levitas, R. (2005) (2nd edn) *The Inclusive Society: social exclusion and New Labour*, Basingstoke, Palgrave Macmillan.
Lewis, A. and Norwich, B. (2005) *Special Teaching for Special Children? Pedagogies for inclusion*, Maidenhead, Open University Press.
Lloyd, G. (2005) *Problem Girls: understanding and supporting troubled and troublesome girls and young women*, London, RoutledgeFalmer.
Lucey, H. (2001) 'Social Class, Gender and Schooling'. In Francis, B. and Skelton, C. (eds) *Investigating Gender: contemporary perspectives in education*, Buckingham, Open University Press.
Mac an Ghaill, M. (1994) *The Making of Men: masculinites, sexualites and schooling*, Buckingham, Open University Press.
Macleod, G. and Munn, P. (2004) 'Social, Emotional and Behavioural Difficulties: a different kind of special educational need?' *Scottish Educational Review*, 36: 2: 169–76.
Macrae, S., Maguire, M. and Millbourne, M. (2003) 'Social Exclusion: exclusion from School', *International Journal of Inclusive Education*, 7: 2: 89–101.
Maguire, M., Macrae, S. and Milbourne, L. (2005) 'Early Interventions: preventing school exclusions in the primary school'. In Rix, J., Simmons, K., Nind, M. and Sheey, K. (eds) *Policy and Power in Inclusive Education: values into practice*, London, RoutledgeFalmer.
Martino W. and Pallotta-Chiarolli (2003) *So What's a Boy? Addressing issues of masculinity and schooling*, Buckingham, Open University Press.
Matthews, R. (2005) 'The Myth of Punitiveness', *Theoretical Criminology*, 9: 2: 175–201.
McCluskey, G. (2008) 'Exclusion from School: what can "included" pupils tell us?' *British Educational Research Journal*, 34: 4: 447–66.
McCluskey, G., Weedon, E., Riddell, S. and Kakos, M. (2008) *Country Notes: Scotland*, Edinburgh, Centre for Research in Education, Inclusion and Diversity, University of Edinburgh.
McDonald, T. and Thomas, G. (2003) 'Parents' Reflections on their Children Being Excluded', *Emotional and Behavioural Difficulties*, 8: 2: 108–19.
McLaughlin, C. (2005) 'Exploring the Psycho-social Landscape of "Problem" Girls: embodiment, relationship and agency'. In Lloyd, G. (Ed) *Problem Girls: understanding and supporting troubled and troublesome girls and young women*, London, RoutledgeFalmer.
McRobbie, A. (1980) 'Settling Accounts with Sub-culture', *Screen Education*, 34: 37–50.
Millbourne, L. (2002) 'Life at the Margin: education of young people, social policy and the meanings of social exclusion', *International Journal of Inclusive Education*, 6: 4: 325–43.
Mills, M. (2001) *Challenging Violence in Schools*, Buckingham and Philadelphia: Open University Press.
Morley, L. and Rassool, N. (1999) *School Effectiveness: fracturing the discourse*, London, Falmer Press.

Mortimore, P. (1999) *The Road to Improvement: reflections on school effectiveness*, Lisse, Swets & Zeitlinger.
Munn, P. and Lloyd, G. (2005) 'Exclusion and Excluded Pupils', *British Educational Research Journal*, 31: 2: 205–21.
Munn, P., Cullen, M. A., Johnstone, M. and Lloyd, G. (1997) *Interchange 47: exclusions and in-school alternatives*, Edinburgh, SOEID.
Munn, P., Lloyd, G. and Cullen, M. A. (2000) *Alternatives to Exclusion from School*, London, Paul Chapman.
Munn, P., Riddell, S., Lloyd, G., Macleod, G., Stead, J., Kane, J. and Fairley, J. (2004) *Evaluation of the Discipline Task Group Recommendations: the deployment of additional staff to promote positive school discipline*, Report to the Scottish Executive.
Nayak, A. (2003) '"Boyz to Men": masculinities, schooling and labour transitions in de-industrial times', *Education Review*, 55: 2: 147–59.
Noble, J. and Davies, P. (2009) 'Cultural Capital as an Explanation of Variation in Participation in Higher Education', *British Journal of Sociology of Education*, 30: 5: 591–605.
O'Connor, W. and Lewis, J. (1999) *Experiences of Social Exclusion in Scotland: research findings number 73*, Edinburgh, Scottish Executive.
Osler, A. and Vincent, K. (2003) *Girls and Exclusion: rethinking the agenda*, London RoutledgeFalmer.
Osler, A., Street, C., Lall, M. and Vincent, K. (2002) *Not a Problem? Girls and school exclusion*, London, National Children's Bureau.
Paechter, C. (1998) *Educating the Other: gender, power and schooling*, London, Falmer Press.
Parsons, C. (1999) *Education, Exclusions and Citizenship*, London, Routledge.
—— (2005) 'School Exclusion: the will to punish', *British Journal of Education Studies*, 53: 2: 187–211.
Phillips, A. (1997) 'From Inequality to Difference: a severe case of displacement?' *New Left Review*, 224: 143–53.
Plummer, G. (2000) *Failing Working-class Girls?* London, Trentham.
Rattansi, A. and Pheonix, A. (1997) 'Re-thinking Youth Identities: modernist and postmodernist frameworks'. In Bynner, J., Chisholm, L. and Furlong, A. (eds) *Youth, Citizenship and Social Change in a European Context*, Aldershot, Ashgate.
Reay, D (1995) '"They Employ Cleaners to Do That": habitus in the primary classroom', *British Journal of Sociology of Education*, 16: 3: 353–71.
—— (1998) *Class Work: mothers' involvement in children's schooling*, London, University College Press.
—— (2001) 'The Paradox of Contemporary Femininities in Education: combining fluidity with fixity'. In Francis, B. and Skelton, C. (eds) *Investigating Gender: contemporary perspectives in education*, Buckingham, Open University Press.
—— (2002) 'Shaun's Story: troubling discourses of white, working-class masculinities', *Gender and Education*, 14: 3: 221–34.
—— (2006) 'The Zombie Stalking English Schools: social class and educational inequality', *British Journal of Educational Studies*, 54: 3: 288–307.
Reay, D. and Wiliam, D. (1999) '"I'll be a Nothing": structure and agency in the construction of identity through assessment', *British Educational Research Journal*, 25: 3: 343–54.
Renold, E. (2004) '"Other" Boys: negotiating non-hegemonic masculinities in the primary school', *Gender and Education*, 16: 2: 247–265.
Riddell, S. (2000) 'Equal Opportunities and Educational Reform in Scotland: the limits of liberalism'. In Salisbury, J. and Riddell, S. (eds) *Gender, Policy and Educational Change: shifting agendas in the UK and Europe*, London, Routledge.

— (2002) *Special Educational Needs*, Edinburgh, Dunedin Academic Press.
Riddell, S. and Banks, P. (2001) *Disability in Scotland: a baseline study*, Strathclyde Centre for Disability Research, University of Glasgow.
Riddell, S. and Tett, L. (2001) *Education, Social Justice and Inter-agency Working: joined up or fractured policy?* London, Routledge.
Ridge, T. (2005) 'Feeling under Pressure: low income girls negotiating school life'. In Lloyd, G. (Ed) *Problem Girls: understanding and supporting troubled and troublesome girls and young women*, London, RoutledgeFalmer.
Rix, J., Simmons, K., Nind, M. and Sheehy, K. (2005) *Policy and Power in Inclusive Education: values into practice*, London, RoutledgeFalmer.
Sammons, P. (1999) *School Effectiveness: coming of age in the twenty first century*, Lisse, Swets & Zeitlinger.
Scottish Education Department (SED) (1978) *The Education of Pupils with Learning Difficulties in Primary and Secondary Schools in Scotland*, Edinburgh, HMSO.
Scottish Executive (1999) *Social Justice . . . a Scotland where everyone matters*, Edinburgh, Scottish Executive.
— (2000) *Standards in Scotland's Schools etc, (Scotland) Act*, Edinburgh, Scottish Executive.
— (2002) *Report of the Cross Party Working Group on Religious Hatred*, Edinburgh, Scottish Executive.
— (2003) *Moving Forward! Additional support for learning*, Edinburgh, Scottish Executive.
— (2004) *A Curriculum for Excellence*, Edinburgh, Scottish Executive.
— (2005) *Statistical Bulletin: Education Series*, Edinburgh, Scottish Executive National Statistics.
— (2007) *Exclusions from School 2005/06*, Edinburgh, National Statistics Publication.
Scottish Executive Education Department (SEED) (2000a) *Better Behaviour – Better Learning*, Edinburgh, Scottish Executive.
— (2000b) *Exclusions from School 1998/99*, Edinburgh, National Statistics Publication.
— (2003) 'Scottish Executive Circular No. 8/03', *Revised Guidance on Issues Concerning Exclusion from School*, Edinburgh, Scottish Executive.
— (2004) *Ambitious, Excellent Schools: our agenda for action*, Edinburgh, Scottish Executive.
— (2005) *Exclusions from School 2003/04*, Edinburgh, National Statistics Publication.
— (2007) *News Release: exclusions from school 2005/2006*, Edinburgh, Scottish Executive.
Scottish Government (2007) *Exclusions from School 2005/06*, Edinburgh, National Statistics Publication.
— (2008) *A Guide to Getting it Right for Every Child*, Edinburgh, Scottish Government: www.scotland.gov.uk/Publications/2008/09/22091734/0. Accessed 31 January 2010.
— (2009a) *Exclusions from School 2007/2008*, Edinburgh, National Statistics Publication.
— (2009b) *Scottish Index of Multiple Deprivation 2009: General Report*, Edinburgh, Scottish Executive: www.scotland.gov.uk/Resource/Doc/151578/0040731.pdf. Accessed 31 January 2010.
Scottish Office (1998) *New Community Schools Prospectus*, Edinburgh, Scottish Office.
Scottish Office Education and Industry Department (SOEID) (1998a) *Circular No. 2/98 Guidance on Issues Concerning Exclusion from School*, Edinburgh, Scottish Office.
— (1998b) *New Community Schools: prospectus*, Edinburgh, Scottish Office.
Silver, H (1994) 'Social Exclusion and Social Solidarity: three paradigms', *International Labour Review*, 133 (5/6): 531–78.
Skeggs, B. (1992) 'Paul Willis, Learning to Labour'. In Barker, M. and Beezer, A. (eds) *Readings into Cultural Studies*, London, Routledge.
— (1997) *Formations of Class and Gender*, London, Sage.

— (2004) *Class, Self, Culture*, London, Routledge.
Skelton, C. (1997) 'Primary Boys and Hegemonic Masculinities', *British Journal of Sociology of Education*, 18: 3: 349–69.
— (2001) *Schooling the Boys*, Buckingham, Open University Press.
Skidmore, D. (2004) *Inclusion: the dynamic of school development*, Maidenhead, Open University Press.
Slee, R., Weiner, G. with Tomlinson, S. (1998) *School Effectiveness for Whom? Challenges to the school effectiveness and improvement movement*, London, Falmer Press.
Spender, D. (1982) *Invisible Women: the schooling scandal*, London, Readers and Writers.
Stead, J., Lloyd, G., Munn, P., Riddell, S., Kane, J. and MacLeod, G. (2007) 'Supporting Our Most Challenging Pupils with Our Lowest Status Staff', *Scottish Education Review*, 39: 2: 186–97.
Stirling, M (1996) 'Government Policy and Disadvantaged Children'. In Blyth, E. and Milner, J. (eds) *Interprofessional Issues for Policy and Practice*, London, Routledge.
Storey, P. and Chamberlin, R. (2001) *Improving the Take Up of Free School Meals*, Norwich, Child Poverty Action Group and Department for Education and the Environment.
Teese, R., Juva, S., Kelly, F. and Van Damme, D. (2007) *Quality and Equity of Schooling in Scotland*, Organisation for Economic Co-operation and Development.
Thomas, G. and Glenny, G. (2000) 'Emotional and Behavioural Difficulties: bogus needs in a false category', *Discourse: studies in the cultural politics of education*, 21: 3: 283–98.
Thomas, G. and Loxley, A. (2001) *Deconstructing Special Education and Constructing Inclusion*, Buckingham, Open University Press.
Thomas, G. and Vaughan, M. (2004) *Inclusive Education: readings and reflections*, Maidenhead, Open University Press.
Tinklin, T. (2003) 'Gender Differences and High Attainment', *British Educational Research Journal*, 29: 3: 308–24.
Tomlinson, S. (2005) (2nd edn) *Education in a Post-welfare Society*, Maidenhead, Open University Press.
UNICEF (2007) *Child Poverty in Perspective: an overview of child well-being in rich countries*, Innocenti Report Card 7, Florence, UNICEF, Innocenti Research Centre.
Viet-Wilson, J. (1998) *Setting Adequacy Standards*, Bristol, Policy Press.
Vincent, C. (2000) *Parents and Teachers: power and participation*, London, Falmer Press.
— (2003) *Social Justice, Education and Identity*, London, RoutledgeFalmer.
Walkerdine, V. (1989) *Counting Girls Out*, London, Virago.
Watson, C. (2005) 'Discourses of Indiscipline: a Foucauldian response', *Emotional and Behavioural Difficulties*, 10: 1: 55–65.
Whitty, G. (2001) *Education, Social Class and Social Exclusion*, London, RoutledgeFalmer.
Willis, P. (1978) *Learning to Labour: why working-class kids get working-class jobs*, London, Saxon House.
Young, I. M. (1990) *Justice and the Politics of Difference*, Princeton, Princeton University Press.

Index

ability 10, 49, 74, 75–7, 79, 82–3, 93; able pupils 15
achievement 45, 63; under-achievement 101 see also attainment
additional support for learning 16; additional support needs 15–16
agency 39, 45–6, 48, 52, 63, 72, 78, 82, 102, 105, 125–8
aggression 61, 70, 72, 73, 105–8; see also violence
anger 89, 107; anger management 85
anti-school behaviour 35; see also resistance model
anti-social behaviour 98, 114; Anti-Social Behaviour Orders 53
army 109
Assertive Discipline 2
assessment 75
aspirations 46, 83
attainment 44, 45, 49, 105, 131–2; raising attainment 19, 21; under-attainment 36, 39, 57, 80, 101
attendance 4, 60; boys' attendance 65, 70, 85; girls' attendance 59, 60, 71, 100, 105
attention deficit hyperactivity disorder (ADHD) 107
attention-seeking behaviour 69
autonomy, of pupils 101, 116 see also control

behaviour monitoring cards 59, 99
behaviour support 59, 90, 112, 130, 135; impact of 85–6; behaviour support bases 59, 85–6, 133
behaviour support teachers 90
Better Behaviour – Better Learning 9, 112, 129, 131
Bourdieuian theory 45–7, 52, 99; of field 46; see also habitus, capitals

boys 2, 37; see also gender, masculinities
bullying 38, 69, 83, 105

capitals 46; cultural capitals 99, 103; social capitals 93, 103
careers 122, 123, 124; see also work (pupils')
case studies 4, 10; construction of 4, 52, Appendix 2
Catholic 55; Catholic denominational education 4, 6, 56, 132
census 5
challenging behaviour 40, 63,79, 84, 100; of boys 35; of girls 54, 59–60
Church of Scotland 4
Children's Hearing System 40; Reporter to Children's Hearings 40
circle time 133
class cultural analyses 9, 34, 45–7; class cultural identities 72
class organisation 79, 81, 90, 121; mixed ability 79, 121; setting 90, 121; 79, streaming 90, 121
classroom space 37, 62; resources 37
class size 80–1
cognitive behaviour therapy 2
college 110
Columbine High School 39
communities 5, 14, 124, 137, community services 64; see also locality, neighbourhood
competition, between schools 20
comprehensive schools 49, 120
conferencing (Restorative) 133
control 65, 72; see also self-control
coordinated support plan (CSP) 15
cooperative teaching 81
crime 14
Criminal Justice (Scotland) Act (2003) 55
cultural affiliations 83

Index   151

cultural transmission 47
curfews 53
curriculum 20, 129, 130–1, 133; alternative curricula 130–1; organisation of 112; planning of 3
Curriculum for Excellence 129

dance 70
depression 62
deprivation 14, 103, 128; areas of deprivation 121; *see also* disadvantage, poverty
deviance 15
dialect 48
differentiation strategies 75
disabilities 8, 46,
disaffection 3; *see also* disengagement
disengagement 17, 39
disobedience 1, 60; *see also* exclusions, reasons for
drugs 59

eating disorders 62
economic decline 5; see also economic decline
Education (Scotland) Act (1918) 4
Education (Additional Support for Learning) (Scotland) Act (2004) and (2009) 15
educational disadvantage 3, 9, 35;
educational inclusion 19; *see also* mainstreaming
Educational Institute of Scotland 37
educational psychologists 69, 96
Eleven Plus 49
embarrassment 102
employment, changes in 18; patterns of employment 44; *see also* labour markets
engagement with schooling *see* participation
England 13, 49
Episcopalian 4
equality 18; *see also* inequality
equal opportunities 37; Equal Opportunities Act (1976) 37
ethnicity 4, 56 ethnic minorities 57
ethnography 43, 50
ethos 3
exclusions, appeals against 24–5; reasons for low rate of appeals 25
exclusions, demography of 2, 4 , 12–13, 53; gender balance of 2; of girls 21, 39–41, 57–62
exclusion, guidelines on 1–2 ; revision of 5;

types of 5, 12, Appendix 1
exclusions, implementation of 1, 2, 29, 115; effects of 26–7, 30; effectiveness of 30–2; period of exclusion 5, 14; purposes of 31–2, 97, 128; tariff system for 29–30, 126; exclusions, parents and 27–8, 30; social class of parents and 28 ; exclusions, policy on 5, 7; comparisons with England 13 ; reductions in 13; target-setting 13
exclusions, pupils perceptions of 23–4, 29–30, 32
exclusion, rates of 1, 2, 12–14;
exclusion, reasons for 1, 8, 50;
exclusion (self-) 71; *see also* truancy
exclusions, schools' perspectives of 2, 32
exclusion, statistics 5; collecting data for 2, 12 ; monitoring of 130; difficulties in collecting data for 13
extra-curricular activities 91, 103

fairness, pupils' perceptions of 29, 126
family 10, 27–8, 50, 83, 91, 95–6, 100–1, 104–5, 116–17, 122; family attitudes 83; responsibility for 91, 100, 104; *see also* parents, fathers, mothers
family support worker 59, 100, 103; *see also* home/school link worker
fathers 65; *see also* parents
femininities 37–42, 57-58, 61–3; 118–20
fighting 106; *see also* aggression and violence
football 69
football support 45, 55, 111; and sectarianism 55–6, 105
free school meals 2, 5, 6, 13–14, 102
friendship 67, 79, 83, 87–91; *see also* peer group

gang fights 55
gender 3, 41; alignments and oppositions 10, 57, 72–3, 119; dichotomies 57, 72; 'types' 41
General Teaching Council 37
Getting it Right for Every Child 16, 128
girls 37–42, 115, 118–19; 'problem' girls 39, 62; *see also* gender and femininities
Glasgow Celtic Football Club 55
Glasgow Rangers Football Club 55
Gypsy/Travellers 15

habitus 46, 52, 78, 99
'hard-to-reach' families 10
health 21

152 Index

Her Majesty's Inspectorate of Education 2
heterosexual attitudes 41
higher education 108, 111; see also university
Highers 83
home/school link worker 70, 71, 86; see also family support worker
homework 23, 26, 98
humour 50, 89
housing scheme 5

identities 35; cultural identities 114; embodied identities 124; identity 'work' 42
inclusive education 14–16, 32, 75–6, 80–1, 131–2
independent schools 49–50
individualised education plan (IEP) 15
industry 6; decline of heavy industry 5
inequality 3, 10, 129, 133; see also social disadvantage
informal exclusion 13, 65, 122, 130, 135
integrated services 17; see also community services
internal exclusion 13, 86

labelling 30, 75–6, 115, 127
labour markets 18; youth labour markets 35, 43–4; 123
ladettes 40–1, 55, 62, 115
laddishness 57
learning difficulties 8, 10, 75, 80, 115
locality 83, 115
'looked after' pupils 2, 111

masculinities 36, 37–9, 117–18; hegemonic 38, 41, 63–4, 67–8, 115, 118; 'problem' 39; working-class; negotiation of working-class 34–5
materialist analyses 35
mainstreaming 2, 14–15, 75–6
media perceptions 2, 8
mental health 21, 64, 122
meritocracy 42, 83
middle-class 35, 46, 68–9
misbehaviour 2; see also challenging behaviour
moshers 53

name-calling 56
National Union of Teachers 37
neds 10, 53–4, 114
neighbourhoods 50, 54; see also communities, locality
New Community Schools 16, 129
New Labour 16
Northern Ireland 49
nurture groups 2

occupations 110; see also careers, work
Orange Walk 55
outcomes of schooling 20

parents 27–9, 95–6, 117; attitudes of 97; control by 96
Parents' Nights 98
participation in the research 4; of parents ;of pupils; of schools 4
participation in schooling 3, 11, 20, 21, 63, 74, 91–2, 103, 113, 126–8; parents' participation in schooling 25–9; 84, 98–9, 122
pedagogies 80–1, 93, 132
peer groups 87–91, 119
peer mediation
Personal and Social Development 85, 88, 133
physical abuse 108
police
poverty 2, 13–14, 17, 21–2, 28–9; 42, 47, 102–5, 122
power 67–8
Presbyterian 4
primary schools 77, 82
professionalism, of teachers 37
Protestant 55
psychiatry 69
public space 103
punishment 9, 23–6; 95, 96
pupil identities 10
pupil support 2, 133
pupil perspectives 21, 30 ; of the future 10; of the research 4
pupil/staff relationships 2, 58, 61, 77, 79, 84–7, 93; respect within 61, 66–7, 87, 126, 133; deference 67

race 43; racism 56–7
Record of Needs 26, 27, 75–6
religion 4
reprisals 55
residential schools
'resistance' model 35, 45; see also anti-school behaviour
Restorative Approaches 2, 98, 133

resources, financial 15
rights, of parents 28; of pupils 26
'risk' society 44
role models 101
Royal Air Force 109

Scottish Executive Education Department (SEED) 7, 26
schools 2; in the research 4–7; mergers 6–7
schooling 115; of identities 48–9, 115–16
school discipline policies 2
school improvement 3, 10, 15–16, 19–20, 35, 43
school organisation 3, 77, 116, 133
school uniform 54, 60–1
Schools of Ambition 129
Scottish Qualifications Agency 130
sectarianism 55, 115
self-awareness 107
self-control 66, 106
self-determination *see* autonomy
self-worth 75
sending home 65, 135 *see also* informal exclusions
setting 49 *see also* class organisation
sexism 37
setting by ability 79, 81, 90 *see also* class organisation
Sex Discrimination Act 37
sexual division of labour 47
siblings 30
special educational needs (SEN) 2, 15–16
special schools and units 14
sport 69, 106
social class 3, 27–9, 43, 99, 114, 117, 120; understandings of; reproduction of 8
social determinism 48
social disadvantage disadvantaged communities ; institutionalised 9; *see also* social exclusion
social division of labour 47
social, emotional and behavioural difficulties (SEBD) 8, 15–16
social exclusion 5, 17; discourses on 19; *see also* social inclusion
social identities 18, 35; multiple identities 39, 53–7; negotiation of social identities 3; politics of 35–7;
social identities, embodiment of 47–9, 58–9

social identities, locality and 44–5, 48
social identities, schooling and 49–50
social inclusion 54, 128; policy on 8,10, 14–19; social inequalities 8, 43, 46, 48
social justice 8, 81, 132
social mobility 131
social work 59, 102
solidarity 89; in the workplace 50
special educational needs 2, 26–7
staff development 129
Standard Grades 71
Standards in Scotland's Schools (Scotland) Act (2000) 14
standpoint 8
streaming 49, 121
stress 42, 116
survival issues 121
swearing 1, 23, 84

teachers 37; skills of 2, 12; professionalism of 66–7
teacher education 11
teaching strategies 75, 79
territorial conflicts 54–5
therapists 15, 26–7
tomboys 39, 55, 61, 115, 119
trades unions 18
transitions 111; primary to secondary 77–8, 93; post-school 20, 35, 43–5, 125
truancy 39, 135; *see also* attendance

university 83, 84; *see also* higher education

value systems 5; of teachers 81, 93; of schools 112
verbal abuse 66, 84
violence 1, 29, 39, 61, 64, 67, 105–8; and girls 61

Wales 49
wealth, distribution of 17
'welfare' approaches 10, 126, 129
welfare regimes 9, 17–18, 103
work 51, 102, 108; pupils' experience of 102;
working class 43, 46; experience of schooling 9, 35; organisations 18

youth culture 10, 53–4; *see also* moshers and neds

eBooks – at www.eBookstore.tandf.co.uk

A library at your fingertips!

eBooks are electronic versions of printed books. You can store them on your PC/laptop or browse them online.

They have advantages for anyone needing rapid access to a wide variety of published, copyright information.

eBooks can help your research by enabling you to bookmark chapters, annotate text and use instant searches to find specific words or phrases. Several eBook files would fit on even a small laptop or PDA.

NEW: Save money by eSubscribing: cheap, online access to any eBook for as long as you need it.

Annual subscription packages

We now offer special low-cost bulk subscriptions to packages of eBooks in certain subject areas. These are available to libraries or to individuals.

For more information please contact webmaster.ebooks@tandf.co.uk

We're continually developing the eBook concept, so keep up to date by visiting the website.

www.eBookstore.tandf.co.uk